BURKE MUSEUM MONOGRAPHS

EXPLORING
COAST SALISH
PREHISTORY

The Archaeology of San Juan Island

JULIE K. STEIN

BURKE MUSEUM OF NATURAL HISTORY AND CULTURE | SEATTLE

UNIVERSITY OF WASHINGTON PRESS | SEATTLE AND LONDON

Library of Congress Cataloging-in-Publication Data

Stein, Julie K.
    Exploring Coast Salish prehistory : the archaeology of San Juan Island / Julie K. Stein.
        p. cm. -- (Burke Museum monograph 8)
    Includes bibliographical references and index.
    ISBN 0-295-97957-7 (alk. paper)
    1. Cattle Point Site (Wash.) 2. English Camp (Wash.) 3. Salish Indians—
Antiquities. 4. Excavations (Archaeology)—Washington (State)—San Juan Island.
5. San Juan Island (Wash.)—Antiquities. 6. San Juan Island National Historical Park
(Wash.)—Antiquities. I. Title. II. Monograph (Thomas Burke Memorial
Washington State Museum) ; 8.

E99.S2 S74 2000
979.7'774--dc21   00-034338

Cover and title page photo:
Unidentified student enrolled in the 1947
University of Washington Archaeology Field School at Cattle Point, WA
(photographer unknown; courtesy of the Burke Museum,
Archaeology Archives)

CONTENTS

PREFACE

This book was written not for archaeologists but for the general public. It exists because of the strong encouragement of Jim Thomson of the National Park Service. I had been working in the San Juan Islands since 1983 and had answered thousands of questions from the general public. Yet every year more people with questions appeared. I gave public presentations of my research every spring, summer, and fall, and new faces emerged time after time. I was finally convinced that these people were asking for a book—written for the general public and not for other archaeologists—that explains through examples what archaeologists actually do, why it is so difficult to piece together the past, and why archaeologists must use every clue, fact, and inference to accomplish it. Countless people have heard me say that archaeologists do not just dig, that most of our effort goes toward piecing together shreds of evidence to construct a past. Excavation is just one way to obtain those pieces. Much more of my time is spent searching countless avenues for other puzzle parts. I was convinced that this message could be effectively presented in a book as well as offered in numerous talks.

So here is that book. Although archaeologists and students may enjoy the contents, it is written for people new to the subject. The story is about the past and based on oral histories, collections from the Burke Museum, historical photos, excavations, and analyses by archaeologists, geologists, paleontologists, foresters, and historians. I hope that the reader will be enlightened by the answers within these pages while acknowledging (as I do) that more questions will always appear.

I would like to thank the many people who helped me bring this information to the public. By far the greatest thanks go to the people within the U.S. National Park Service (NPS). Four superintendents have allowed me to conduct research within the park: Frank Hastings (1983–85), Dick Hoffman (1985–89), Robert Scott (1990–98), and Cicely Muldoon (1999–present). Jim Thomson, the regional archaeologist, and Kent Bush, the regional curator, have encouraged and educated me for more than ten years. Recently, Camille Evans, the past curator for the San Juan Island National Historical Park, has helped me with the collections from Cattle Point and the early excavations of English Camp. Mike Vouri and Dr. Wayne Suttles assisted with historical references, which helped greatly. Steve Gobat, Bill Gleason, and Shirley Hole, all working at the San Juan Island National Historical Park, have helped make my work easier. A special thanks to Steve Kenady, who through the generosity of the Park Service was able to provide me with much information about his excavation.

Many people contributed greatly to this project, including Patty Rasmussen who still cooks for us and houses us whenever we return to the island for more information. Eric Rasmussen assists with data collection, curation, drafting, and electrical and mechanical needs. Rick Hilton, our personal computer consultant, can make the catalog do whatever is required. Walter Bartholomew cataloged and computerized most of the English Camp and Cattle Point collections. His attention to detail is appreciated.

Students at the University of Washington excavated the English Camp site through many field schools, and I have thanked most of them elsewhere. Most important are the students who have conducted research on these collections, allowing me to write this summary. Margaret Nelson, Pamela Ford, Fran (Whittaker) Hamilton, Kim Kornbacher, Tim Latas, Ed Bakewell, Robert Bohus, Tim Hunt, Mark Madsen, Angela Linse, Sarah Sherwood, Diana Greenlee, Debbie Bradley, Elizabeth Martinson, Lance Lundquist, Ethan Cochrane, MaryAnn Emery, Kristine Bovy, Gregg Sullivan, Brian Pegg, and Debby Green have all contributed significantly to the archaeology of the Northwest. Their work allows me to write this story.

Without a doubt there are two people who have helped me most in the completion of this book. Mary Parr directed the laboratory at the excavation, oversaw the sorting, cataloging, computerizing, and curation of all 50,000 objects in the years following the excavation, and acts as our collective memory for all aspects of this project. Mary encouraged me to complete this book, offering editorial comments as well as conducting (with MaryAnn Emery) the needed photographic research and processing. She has been with me on this project for so long that we can no longer tell whose ideas are whose. Laura Phillips is the collections manager at the Burke Museum and since 1994 has overseen the NPS collections. Her computer genius is responsible for all the graphics in this book, and she helped immensely with what I have written. The contributions of these two colleagues and friends have made this book possible.

Thanks to Mary Parr, Laura Phillips, and the many other people who helped me with the photography appearing in this book: Jennie Deo, Kris Bovy, Arn Slettebak, Melissa Parr, Elizabeth Scharf, Steven Denton, and Nancy Morningstar.

I would like to acknowledge the gracious advice of two members of the Lummi Indian Nation, Sts'aStelQuyd (Al Scott Johnnie), director of the Lummi Schelangen Department, and Tsi'li'xw (Bill James), language instructor. Although archaeologists and Native Americans have not always agreed on their interpretations of the past, these two individuals took the time to read an archaeologist's words. I thank them for all of their suggestions, especially those providing more appropriate phrasing. I also would like to thank the Lummi Indian Nation for permission to quote their elders.

This manuscript was reviewed by Jim Thomson, Dr. Karl Hutterer, Gary Wessen, Mary Parr, Laura Phillips, MaryAnn Emery, Suzanne Lebsock, Christopher Lockwood, and Stan Chernicoff. The index was expertly prepared by Christopher Lockwood. I am grateful for all of their comments and assistance.

Exploring Coast Salish Prehistory

The Archaeology of San Juan Island

INTRODUCTION

The San Juan Islands of Washington State have been the homeland of people for thousands of years. Modern visitors to the islands notice shells eroding from a bank or spreading across a beach and envision scenarios of life long ago before the conveniences of electricity and plumbing. Who were the people who dropped these shells? How long ago did they stand in this spot?

Attempting to answer those questions is at once exciting and frustrating. Evidence about the past comes in two forms: the physical remains left on the landscape and picked up by archaeologists, and the observations recorded as historical impressions in journals or as part of the oral heritage of Native Americans. These two forms, remains and observations, provide different kinds of information. One (archaeological) helps us trace the people's actual movements, but is silent about the significance of those movements or the motivations behind them. The other (historical) is the summation of people's recollections of a society's rules and motivations.

The past depicted in this book comes from the study of the physical remains found in the ground, or archaeology. But this book also includes observations and oral histories of native peoples, ethnographers, and explorers. The historical information is offered to illustrate the limits of archaeology. Archaeology can give us only things, not thoughts. Anyone can conjure romantic or exotic depictions of the past and explore the motivations behind actions, technological inventions, or architectural features. The thoughts or motives of people living thousands of years ago have long since vanished. As modern visitors sit on the beach in the San Juan Islands, imaginations run free, but what we actually know about the past comes from the shells before us.

The written heritage of local peoples suggests that within the last few hundred years, people moved about the mainland and islands, collecting resources, visiting other villages, and trading. They owned resources in vastly distant locations: a shellbed on Orcas Island, a camas field on San Juan Island, a reef-net location near Point Roberts. They did not own a tract of land as we do today. Their kinship, property, and subsistence systems were sophisticated and markedly different from those of the Europeans who first encountered and tried to understand them.

The Native American peoples currently living in the Northwest are the descendants of people who have lived in the area for thousands of years. Archaeology is the study of human behavior on the basis of the objects left by forebears, and the archaeology of the San Juan Islands employs the objects left by people over many thousands of years to understand and reconstruct early cultures. We must look to the living descendants of the people to obtain that understanding. Many of the objects from the past are recognizable to the people of today. Some, however, were made and used so long ago that none of us is sure of their meaning or function. Until the time machine is invented we will have to settle for the bits and pieces of information found in oral histories and archaeological sites. This book presents the knowledge that we have gathered thus far.

The San Juan and Gulf islands are part of the Gulf of Georgia Culture Area, a term used by archaeologists to designate the region between Vancouver Island and the mainland of Washington and British Columbia. The archaeological sites in this culture area contain similar artifacts and share similar physical characteristics, such as the presence of shell, abundant charcoal, and rock that is cracked by fire. In this region today, native languages are similar to one another and people share many religious beliefs. Differences in culture do exist across the various landforms in the Gulf of Georgia Culture Area, but there are many more commonalities.

A number of sites within the Gulf of Georgia Culture Area have been examined by archaeologists. This book will focus on two of these locations. Both lie within the boundaries of the San Juan Island National Historical Park, and together they offer a wide variety of items and features, allowing us a partial view of the rich cultural heritage of

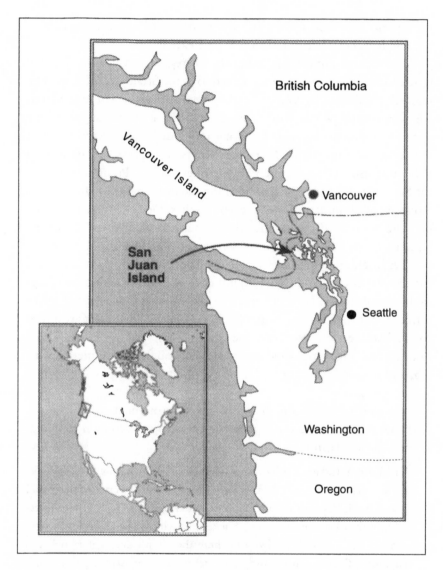

The San Juan islands are located northwest of Puget Sound and northeast of the Strait of Juan de Fuca. Other islands in the same group but across the Canadian border are called the Gulf Islands. Archaeologists refer to the entire region as the Gulf of Georgia Culture Area.

the region as a whole. Other sites will be discussed in this presentation, but few have been excavated to the same extent.

The Native Americans living in the region today speak Central Coast Salish languages and are referred to as the Strait Coast Salish. The research conducted by Wayne Suttles suggests that the San Juan Islands are occupied by people who speak the Northern Straits language, one of five component languages making up Central Coast Salish. Before the arrival of Europeans, Northern Straits was spoken by people on Vancouver Island from Saanich Inlet to Sherringham Point, throughout the San Juan and Gulf islands, and along the mainland shore from Point Roberts and Boundary Bay to Deception Pass. Descendants of the people who once lived throughout this area are modern members of the Songhees, Saanich, Lummi, and Samish tribes and nations.

Tribal elders remember when their people lived in the San Juan Islands year-round, and they remember moving their winter dwellings to the mainland. Today they return to the San Juan Islands to fish every summer, but they can no longer freely collect shellfish, camas roots, or native blackberries. Nor can they hunt deer, elk, or birds. These resources have been depleted or destroyed through development, farming, and livestock grazing, and access to them is often blocked by private ownership.

Herman Olsen (born in 1909), an elder of the Lummi Nation, describes what happened to native people who used to own resources in the San Juan Islands.

> The Lummi Indians can't even go ashore on San Juan now to dig a bucketful of clams. They get drove away. There are only a very few beaches. I know Birch Bay you're only allowed so many clams. They're big hearted too; they let us go and get a bucketful anyhow, but up around where the old Lummis used to live out there they don't even get a bucketful anymore. They get drove away even before they get started. They won't even let you land a boat anymore in lots of the old places. (*Lummi Elders Speak,* p. 66)

Although these Native Americans flourish in a twentieth-century world, they maintain traditions that reflect their millennia in the San Juan Islands. They speak knowledgeably about their heritage, and much of what archaeologists hypothesize about the past is based on the knowledge of these people.

This book is written by an archaeologist and will represent the archaeological perspective, but it does not suggest that other perspectives are invalid. The native perspective presents longstanding cultural traditions, deeply rooted in belief systems, and awareness of the world around us. Each perspective can be defended with abundant facts, and each explains the world in which we live.

SAN JUAN ISLAND NATIONAL HISTORICAL PARK

Within the boundaries of the San Juan Island National Historical Park, many locations that are important to Native Americans today show signs of having been important in the past. The Lummi, Saanich, Samish, and Songhees have indicated to Suttles the locations of winter villages and summer camps in the San Juan Islands. Archaeologists have identified hundreds of other places in the San Juan Islands where people lived and camped over the millennia. Some archaeological sites are located in places remembered by the descendants of the original occupants; others are not. Two archaeological sites are located within the National Historical Park and have been examined extensively by archaeologists.

The Pig War

The National Historical Park was created to preserve not these archaeological sites but locations of more recent historical events surrounding the establishment in 1846 of the international boundary between the United States and Canada. The boundary was established as the middle of the channel that separates Vancouver Island from the mainland. This boundary description was immediately disputed, for two channels divide Vancouver Island from the mainland, with the San Juan Islands falling between. Immediately after the international boundary was established, both the British and the Americans claimed the San Juan Islands for themselves. Each country had citizens living on the islands, and the British Hudson's Bay Company had a farm located at San Juan Island's southern end.

The historian Erwin Thompson summarizes the events leading to the boundary dispute. On June 15, 1859, an American settler named Cutler shot and killed a pig belonging to the Hudson's Bay Company. The pig had escaped, not for the first time, and was rooting in Cutler's garden. When the British discovered the dead pig they threatened to arrest Cutler. The Americans living on the island demanded military protection from the angry British. In response to the threat of an attack by the British, the American Brigadier General William S. Harney sent a company of U.S. infantry to San Juan Island. The British countered by sending three British warships and British Royal Marines. (See book by Michael Vouri for details of this military event.) The standoff that ensued has been called "The Pig War."

The crisis was not resolved for more than a decade, during which time both the British and the Americans established encampments. The British camp was located on the northwest side of the island, at Garrison Bay, and the Americans' at the southern end of the island, near the old Hudson's Bay Company farm and the spit of land called Cattle Point. Soldiers occupied these garrisons for twelve years with no official duties other than to occupy the disputed territory. Finally, in 1872 Kaiser Wilhelm I of Germany, an arbitrator chosen to settle the issue, ruled in favor of the United States, establishing the boundary line through Haro Strait, the western channel. The San Juan Islands were confirmed as American territory, and the British troops withdrew.

The National Historical Park was created in 1966 to preserve the historic army campsites; as fortune had it, two large prehistoric sites were thus also preserved. (The term historic is here used to describe events after the arrival of Europeans to the Northwest Coast; during this period events were recorded in writing. The term prehistoric refers to the time before contact with Europeans or European trade goods, our knowledge of which comes from archaeological records and oral histories.)

Sites

The two prehistoric sites preserved within the boundaries of the San Juan Island National Historical Park are Cattle Point (45SJ1) and English Camp (45SJ24). Archaeological sites in the United States are given both names and codes to designate them as unique locations. Each number and letter of the code provides information about the site's location. All the contiguous states are numbered in alphabetical order; Washington is number forty-five. Each county within a state is assigned an official abbreviation; San Juan County is SJ. Finally, each site is officially recorded in the Washington State Office of Archaeology and Historic Preservation in Olympia and given a number ordered sequentially within each county. Cattle Point was the very first site recorded in San Juan County, and English Camp was the twenty-fourth. Thus, the number 45SJ1 indicates that Cattle Point is the first recorded site in San Juan County in the state of Washington. The name given to sites is designated by the archaeologist who records the site; it is usually the surname of the landowner or the name of a nearby landform.

EXCAVATIONS

The older of the two sites within the park is Cattle Point. It was excavated twice, first in 1946–47 under the direction of Dr. Arden King, who was teaching a field school for the University of Washington (he was a faculty member at Tulane University in New Orleans). Dr. Carroll Burroughs (an archaeologist working for the National Park Service at Mesa Verde who came to teach the field school for the University of Washington) directed the second excavation in 1948. In 1950 King published a report in *American Antiquity* (the journal of the Society for American Archaeology) summarizing the results of both excavations.

The second site is English Camp (45SJ24), excavated three times. In 1950, Dr. Adan E. Treganza (from San Francisco State University) taught a field school for the University of Washington there. In 1970–72, Dr. Roderick Sprague, an archaeologist from the University of Idaho specializing in the historic period, directed a large excavation. He was assisted by an archaeologist responsible for the prehistoric aspects of the site, Stephen Kenady, who was then a student at the University of Washington. Sprague published his results in many reports and articles, but he best summarized his findings in the two-volume publication *San Juan Archaeology*, published by the National Park Service in 1983. I led the third and most recent investigation from 1983 to 1991 directing field schools from the University of Washington. I published my results in *Deciphering a Shell Midden*, published by Academic Press in 1992.

The name of Site 45SJ24 is problematic for an interesting historical reason. Among British soldiers who garrisoned the camp, there were men from Wales, Scotland, and Ireland, as well as from England; to include everyone, they referred to themselves as British, not English. After the soldiers left San Juan Island, the American settlers of the island were deaf to those distinctions and habitually referred to the place of British occupation as English Camp. After 1966 the National Park Service restored the historically accurate name British Camp. The local people of San Juan Island objected to this name and filed a grievance with the Department of Interior's Domestic Geographic Board. The board upheld the name favored by the locals, and the name was changed back to English Camp. For this reason, in stories and articles

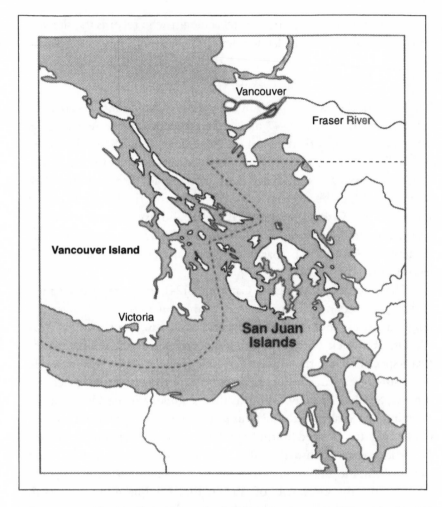

The San Juan islands include 3 large islands (San Juan, Lopez, and Orcas), at least 5 medium-sized islands (Shaw, Decatur, Blakely, Cypress, Waldron), and nearly 200 smaller islands.

published about this location, both English and British Camp are seen. They are, however, the same place.

Both sites are shell middens. The word *midden* is derived from a Danish word meaning "material that accumulates around a dwelling." Archaeologists use midden to refer to areas that have an abundance of tools, mixed with other evidence of people's subsistence, technology, dwellings, and refuse. The objects in a midden are called *artifacts,* and middens usually are characterized by thick concentrations of artifacts, the most abundant of which is shell. When a midden contains shell, it is referred to as a *shell midden*. Cattle Point is a shell midden deposited on a sandy gravel ridge above a beach. It has little forest cover and is exposed to high winds and erosion. In contrast, English Camp is a shell midden deposited on a quiet muddy shoreline. English Camp has suffered some erosion and infilling of the bay, and there is abundant forest cover.

These sites show evidence of thousands of years of occupation, continuing up through the historic period. English Camp may have been in use as a winter village when the British soldiers arrived in 1859. On the other hand, Cattle Point has not been identified specifically as the location of either a winter village or summer fishing spot by Native American tribal elders. Evidently the spot is no longer remembered. The artifacts, however, testify to the use of the location, remembered or not. This is a good example of why archaeological, historical, and ethnographic information are all crucial. The Cattle Point site contains material suggesting that summer fishing and gathering activities took place there.

How Archaeologists Reconstruct the Past

Archaeologists in the Northwest have created what we call a culture history of the area. They have done this over the last 100 years and follow a method influenced strongly by an anthropologist who worked from the 1850s to 1900, Franz Boas. Boas proposed that cultures be described by condensing them into "generalized patterns of behavior." He believed that all human behavior could be seen as modal patterns enforced by a set of rules defined in the culture. This theory is referred to as *the normative concept of culture*. The rules are passed from one generation to the next, some within the family, others within schools or occupations. Some behavior is idiosyncratic, but most is regulated by norms.

Norms in this context are really ranges of behaviors. Each range represents only a portion of the potential behaviors. Anything outside that range is considered deviance, which in turn is regulated in a variety of ways. For example, in the United States, what clothing is considered appropriate to wear to a traditional wedding ceremony? Would you wear blue jeans, khaki shorts, or a bathing suit? If you did, how would other people react? Would you be arrested, thrown in jail, or just the object of stares and whispers? Within our society there are ranges of acceptable behaviors that are enforced through subtle (and not so subtle) social pressures. Boas used these norms as the basis of his culture concept.

Boas and other anthropologists divided the world into *cultural areas*. These areas were defined by historical observations and ethnographies. Cultural groups were classified on the basis of language, physical and cultural characteristics, and material culture (the objects made and used).

Archaeologists make use of the normative view of culture to reconstruct or describe the nature and sequence of past behavior. The remains of past cultures recovered by archaeologists, such as tools and other material goods, are assumed to represent past behavioral norms. This method reduces artifacts into slices of time: each slice of time is a period when people followed a particular set of standard rules.

The archaeological method of finding norms requires that archaeologists group all artifacts that are alike into categories called types. A *type* (the perfect behavior or modal behavior) is a class of object defined by a consistent clustering of attributes. Archaeologists build sequences of time by stacking younger types on top of older types. For example, leaf-shaped points are older than triangular-shaped points.

After a type is defined, the next step is to group all the different types into components. A *component* is an association of all the artifacts from one level at a site. So all the artifact types from one portion of the site are placed together and called one component. For example, leaf-shaped points are often found with cobble tools and together would be referred to as component #1 in a site.

The next step is to move beyond the single site and build a comparative chronology by grouping all the types and components of groups of sites into a phase. A *phase* represents similar components from more than one site. A phase is thought of as a culture or occupation and represents time and occupation over space. A phase in reality is a group of types—a component found over a large area. Archaeologists use the normative culture concept to interpret these similar artifacts as people walking over the landscape at a specific time, doing specific (normal) things. One problem with phases, however, is that the archaeologist never knows what the normal behavior or region really was. So types are often found in different sites in different combinations. Recently, archaeologists have turned to radiocarbon dating instead of types and components alone.

Once the phase is identified, the archaeologist uses radiocarbon dating to define the range of dates over which a phase existed, and then constructs a culture history. A *culture history* is a sequence of time and types constructed for each culture area. The sequence is manageable in terms of time and space and convenient units in which archaeologists can study the past. Although radiocarbon dates are replacing the phases as a system for sorting types, phase names continue to be used as a short cut to tell time.

Archaeologists would like to know more than just a culture history for a culture area. Artifacts and types should be brought to life and should offer explanations for changes that we detect. That leap of logic, from the artifacts we find to reconstructing and interpreting what they mean, requires bridging arguments. The most common ones are based on analogy, culture ecology, and evolution.

Ethnographic and historic analogy uses the observations made by anthropologists, historians, and explorers, and the oral histories of native peoples to interpret the functions of objects found in an archaeological context. This method works well for artifacts found in sites that have been occupied recently. The chances of the object being used the same way in both the archaeological context and the ethnographic or historic one are high. Problems arise when comparisons are made between people living today and people living thousands of years ago. The chances are not as high that the function of objects will be the same in both periods. In fact, the objects found in the older sites usually have no modern analog in any description or recollection.

Another method is to use common sense or experimentation to interpret function. If the object has a sharp edge, then it stands to reason that it was probably used to chop or cut something. One tries cutting various materials and sees which is cut most efficiently. The problem with this method is that the true function is not verified just because the experimenter has found an efficient use for an item. The original maker may have made the object for a task that the experimenter had not even thought to test.

Neither of these methods for interpreting the past explains why the object's shape or function changed. *Culture ecology* emphasizes the interdependence of people's behavior and their environment. If the environment changes, then people change behaviors in order to survive. Archaeologists sometimes look to geologists or climatologists for evidence of an environmental change coincident with an artifact change. Often, however, no correlations are found.

The second method for explaining changes in the past is *evolution*. People have a great deal of variability in why and how they do things. Within that variability some things will allow the individual or group to reproduce more often and have a greater number of offspring that adapt quickly to outside pressures. Those behaviors that promote success will be naturally selected. Darwin noted this variability in species and used it to explain change in biological evolution. The suggestion here is that the same principles operate in cultural systems. Disagreement exists on the nature of the transmission—culturally learned as opposed to biologically transmitted through genes—but overall similarities seem to exist between the two methods. One problem for people trying to use evolution in archaeology is that the Boasian approach, which emphasizes tallying objects in terms of central tendencies or norms, cannot be adapted to tallying the variability in the assemblage. For example, if scrapers were made in a variety of sizes, grouping them into two categories of larger than 5 cm and smaller than 5 cm would emphasize the normal sizes of scrapers and de-emphasize the variability in scraper sizes. Evolution requires that variability be examined in each artifact type of each site, and archaeologists have (for at least 100 years) been reducing that variability into normative types. Evolution is a new and powerful tool that many researchers are using to explain why changes occurred.

On the Northwest Coast, archaeologists have been using primarily two approaches, culture ecology and culture history. In fact, so few sites have been excavated and so little radiocarbon dating has been done that we still have disagreements about the components and phases, the environmental events that may have influenced people living in the region, and the variability across the region and within the site. The problem for archaeologists in the Northwest is that the shell middens here are extremely difficult to excavate. They are too big and complex to excavate quickly. They contain abundant fish, shellfish, plant remains, and sediment that must be sampled and saved. They contain few objects that offer information about style, function, technology, or change, so large areas of the site have to be excavated to get sufficient samples. We know less about the prehistoric past of the Northwest than about that of other regions, but we are catching up rapidly, as you are about to see.

CATTLE POINT SITE

The Cattle Point site (45SJ1) is located two miles west of the prominent landform labeled on maps as Cattle Point. The archaeological site stretches for several hundred meters along the top of the bluff above the beach, as well as along the lower beach. Three natural springs emerge at the base of the bluff in the vicinity of the site. The springs and the presence of an offshore bank over which migrating salmon must swim made this location an attractive spot for fishing, shellfishing, and gathering roots, and therefore for prehistoric occupation. Most evidence suggests that this site was seasonally occupied, especially during the summer salmon runs.

THE AGE OF THE
CATTLE POINT SHELL MIDDEN

When Arden King excavated the Cattle Point site, he believed that people had been there for thousands of years and that over time the traditions of these people changed. He thought that the history of these people could be roughly divided into four phases based on the kind of animal remains he found in the site and on the tools the people left behind. Interestingly, King defined phases rather than components, yet his excavation was the first in the region and was not a comparison of artifact types across a region. (Components are defined at one site, and phases are similar components at more than one site.) King proposed the phases as a starting point, to be refined after archaeologists excavated other sites.

Arden King encountered deposits that he believed dated from 5,000 year ago through nearly the present, and he placed his depositional layers into phases that he called the *Island, Developmental, Maritime,* and *Late Phases.* According to him, Island and Developmental Phases extended from approximately 9,000 to 2,500 years ago, with the Maritime and Late Phases following and lasting until about 200 years ago.

Archaeologists who were contemporaries of King's, and those who followed him, do not use King's phase names when discussing the prehistory of the Northwest Coast. Dr. Charles Borden of the University of British Columbia excavated sites along the Fraser River at the same time King excavated Cattle Point and developed a different sequence. Borden published his sequence for the Fraser River chronology in 1950, the same year that King published his for Cattle Point. For a number of reasons (having mostly to do with Borden's forceful personality and scholarship) Borden's sequence (as revised by Dr. Roy Carlson of Simon Fraser University, Dr. Donald Mitchell of University of Victoria, and Dr. David Burley of Simon Fraser University) was accepted and used, while King's was ignored.

CHRONOLOGY OF SOUTHERN NORTHWEST COAST				
Years Ago	Years A.D./B.C.	King's Term	Characteristics	New Terms
Present — 2000 A.D.				
		Late Phase	Shell Fewer artfacts	San Juan Phase
1500 — 500 A.D.				
		Maritime Phase	Abundant shell Variety of artifacts Triangular and stemmed points	Marpole Phase
2500 — 500 B.C.				
		Developmental Phase	Shell Fish, bird, and terrestrial mammals Bone tools Stemmed points	Locarno Beach Mayne/ St. Mungo Phases
4500 — 2500 B.C.				
		Island Phase	Absence of shell Terrestrial mammals Leaf-shaped points	Cascade Phase
9000 — 7000 B.C.				
11,500	9500 B.C.	—	Makers of Clovis points None found in San Juan Islands	Paleoindian Period

The time of the earliest occupation of western Washington is referred to as the Paleoindian period, represented by the appearance of the Clovis point. Clovis points are distinctively shaped stone tools thought to have been attached to handles or shafts and used as knives or spears. No Clovis points have been found in the San Juan Islands or on any islands to the north. To the south, however, one Clovis point has been found on Whidbey Island, and others have been found at locations along southern Puget Sound.

These people are believed to have come into North America across the Bering Land Bridge about 11,500 years ago, and they made their distinctive points for about 500 years. (King did not find any of these at Cattle Point, so he did not include this period in his sequence.) Very little is known about the people of this period in the San Juan Islands. The glaciers had receded and land was exposed above sea level, but no sites or artifacts from this time have been recovered in the San Juan Islands. Archaeologists have suggested that the people were adjusting to the changing climate and landscape associated with the end of the Pleistocene epoch.

It is noteworthy that Native Americans do not believe that people came into North America over the Bering Land Bridge. They know that their ancestors have always occupied this land. Their origin myths take place here in the San Juan Islands, not on some other continent. Archaeologists and Native Americans diverge widely on this issue, and it is up to each reader to decide his/her own beliefs.

1. The Cascade Phase. What we know of the earliest occupation at Cattle Point (and in the islands and region) is based on the objects found in the deepest layers of the site. In those layers no shell was found, but artifacts were found indicating that people did live here. This ancient soil is still preserved below ground, and it indicates that the grassland habitat of American Camp developed long ago and has remained much the same over the last few thousand years.

From the artifacts and animal bones in these lowest layers, King reconstructed this phase as a time when people exploited terrestrial resources (those found on the land) to the exclusion of marine resources (those found in salt water). He believed that these early occupants of the islands hunted animals on the land, collected plants, and drank fresh water, but they did not (at this location) leave any remains of fish or shellfish. King did find some mammal bones (their size suggests that they came from deer and elk), so people were bringing animal remains back to Cattle Point. The preservation of these bones is unusual because most Northwest soils are acidic and do not encourage bone preservation. The buried soil at Cattle Point, developed in the sandy substrate laid down by the glaciers, must be less acidic than soils in other areas.

Difficult as it may be for us to accept, people living at Cattle Point during this time did not rely on marine resources. Sites on the Fraser and Columbia Rivers suggest that people there were collecting some salmon during this phase. Salmon vertebrae are sometimes found at these river sites, but even when no bones are preserved the very locations of the sites suggest a focus on river resources. Yet salmon fishing in a river is not the same as fishing in open water. The people in the San Juans were most likely not fishing, collecting abundant shellfish, or hunting marine mammals at this time.

During this early period, the people of the San Juans made points in the shape of a willow leaf, with points on both ends, a style considered old in this part of the world. The word *point* is used by archaeologists instead of *arrowhead* or *knife* because no one knows exactly the function of these pointed tools. The leaf-shaped points found at Cattle Point are made of dacite, a fine-grained, black volcanic rock, the source of which was most likely coastal British Columbia. These points may have been used as the tips of spears or as knives.

King called this early period the *Island Phase,* since economic life was adapted to land rather than sea resources. He did not have any technique to help him determine the age of this early occupation, but on the basis of the deeply buried position and the presence of leaf-shaped points he guessed that the people who left this material did so 5,000 years ago. We now have techniques to determine the age of charcoal and other organic matter, but King did not save charcoal when he excavated this lowest layer in the site. Other sites with such points have been found with charcoal that dates from 9,000 to 4,500 years ago.

The phase name used most frequently today is not King's *Island Phase,* but rather the *Cascade Phase* (also called the *Early Period* and the *Old Cordilleran Culture Type*). It is characterized by the presence of Cascade points and other leaf-shaped points made 9,000 to 4,500 years ago. Some of the leaf-shaped points have been found in sites that may be as young as 3,000 years old, indicating that the style remained popular after the Cascade Phase ended. People living during this phase are thought to have relied mainly on terrestrial resources. This conclusion, however, is based on the location of these sites far from shorelines and close to places good for hunting deer or elk. This idea is difficult to test because the sites we see today that are from the Cascade Phase contain few animal remains. As glaciers slowly melted, the sea level rose, inundating coastlines all over the world. About 5,000 years ago, the sea level stabilized.

If people were collecting resources at the shore, the sites they used would now be under water. The only sites we find from Cascade Phase occupations are above today's shorelines and lack (for the most part) any evidence of marine resources. The evidence suggests that these early inhabitants of the region, successors of the Clovis people, were focused on land resources and not those of the sea. Such people may have been living at the Cattle Point site for short periods of time, leaving just a few objects and remains, and the shoreline may have been located farther out to sea.

2. The St. Mungo, Mayne, and Locarno Beach Phases. The second phase that King recognized is distinguished by the appearance of shell; he called it the *Developmental Phase*. Archaeologists have now divided King's phase into two or three phases because we have more information than King had. On top of the oldest layers, King found strata that contained the remains of shellfish such as clams, mussels, and barnacles. The shells of these organisms are made of calcium carbonate, a mineral that changes the chemistry of the soil from acid to alkaline and helps in the process of preserving bone. Bones were preserved below the shell in deposits dated to the Cascade Phase, so the Cattle Point soils may not have been originally acidic. The presence of shell, however, ensured the preservation of bone in all sites across the Northwest, even in locations where soil acidity was high before occupation.

Along with the shell, King found the bones of fish, birds, and land mammals. The first shellfish to be deposited were mussels, seemingly the preference of the people who first relied on marine resources at this and other sites in the San Juan Islands. Other shellfish were later added to the diet. The layers at Cattle Point, from the St. Mungo, Mayne, and Locarno Beach Phases, contain clams and barnacles, as well as mussels in the upper layers of the phase. The layers from this phase were the first to contain shellfish remains, so King believed that it was during this time period that people first relied on marine resources and exploited them extensively.

The artifacts found in these layers include tools made of bone and a new kind of stone point with a stem. Stems appear on stone points, perhaps to improve the strength of the attachment of the point to the handle (or spear shaft) or perhaps as a stylistic change that gained in popularity. For example, the basic function of a hammer has not changed for thousands of years, but the style of hammers has changed. Some changes reflect technological innovation; others are stylistic ones. The stems on points appear to have both functional and stylistic advantages.

Arden King found three types of points at the Cattle Point site. The leaf-shaped points from the oldest layers are thought to be from 9,000 to 4,500 years old. The stemmed points from the middle layers are thought to be 4,500 to 1,500 years old, and the triangular points (overlapping in time with the stemmed points) from the upper layers roughly 2,500 to 200 years old. The base of a point is shaped in different ways so as to attach it (or haft it) to a handle, spear shaft, or arrow. People change the shape of the base according to the task that they wish to perform and the style that is popular. These shapes are used by archaeologists to tell relative time. (Photograph by Nancy Morningstar)

King believed that the shell layers of the Cattle Point site were between 5,000 and 1,500 years old. Luckily, King saved some of the shells and stored them at the Burke Museum. In 1974 they were submitted to radiocarbon analysis. From this we now know that the shells were extracted from the shore between 2,500 and 2,300 years ago, indicating that the shell layers were deposited at that time. Comparable dates have been recorded at the Sequim Bypass site, located across the Strait of Juan de Fuca, where similar artifacts were found. Stemmed points and shellfish have been found in quite a few sites where ages of charcoal and shellfish fall within that interval of time. So archaeologists believe that King's guesses were on the mark.

The phase name used most frequently today is not King's Developmental Phase, but rather the St. Mungo, Mayne, and Locarno Beach Phases. These phases follow the Cascade Phase and persist for the period of time from roughly 4,500 to 2,500 years ago. The Locarno Beach Phase is by far the best known and represented in most sites. The St. Mungo Phase may be represented by people living primarily on the mainland, and the Mayne Phase is an early version of the Locarno Beach Phase found in the island setting. (Donald Mitchell, an archaeologist at the University of Victoria, suggested in 1971 that the Mayne Phase is the same as the Locarno Beach Phase.) The period of time represented by these phases is indicated by deposits containing projectile points with stems and slate knives. The sites of this age are found near the shore-lines—indicating that people expanded their subsistence to include marine resources, especially shellfish—and contain both bone and chipped stone objects. Through time, the people made more and more complex bone implements and carved bone and stone pieces, expanding the intricacy of design in their manufacturing technique and style.

Among the new inventions were woodworking tools such as large stone mauls, adzes, and wedges, found in deposits thought to date from this time period. The appearance and increase in the number of these tools may be associated with the arrival and establishment of mature western red cedar forests. The earliest cedar pollen found in the San Juan Island region dates from around 4,000 years ago. It is hard for us to imagine the Northwest without large cedar forests, but it was people living during the St. Mungo and Locarno Beach Phases who first wit-nessed the appearance of the mature cedar and Douglas fir forests and who eventually established a thriving culture based on this ecosystem.

Archaeologists have suggested that between 4,500 and 2,500 years ago, the complexity of people's organizational structure, arts, and tech-nology increased as changes in landscape, plants, and animals occurred. At the end of the Locarno Beach Phase and during the succeeding Marpole Phase there was a rapid increase in the exploitation of cedar, including for the first time its use for such things as plank houses and clothing. The characteristic Northwest Coast culture adaptations to shorelines, wetlands, forests, and mountains most likely began during the Marpole Phase around 2,500 years ago.

3. The Marpole Phase. The third group of layers (those close to what is now the surface) contained abundant shells and a wide variety of tools, including another new kind of stone point: the triangular point. King thought that the people who left the material in these layers were exploiting marine resources more than ever before. He called the period the *Maritime Phase*.

King believed that the increased use of shellfish may have been only in part a matter of preference. He felt that a more likely explanation was that the configuration of the beach had changed to promote the growth of more shellfish beds. In other words, people did not wake up one day and feel like eating great quantities of shellfish and do so for the next few hundred years; rather, changes in the environment led to greater shellfish availability at the site.

The configuration of the shore changed because the sea level rose and currents on this part of the island eroded the bluffs to the east, moving the sand to the west and filling in small bays along the way. The sand provided the habitats in which shellfish flourished, and once the shellfish multiplied, people came to collect and process them.

The phase name used most frequently today is not King's *Maritime Phase,* but rather the Marpole Phase. Around 2,500 to 1,500 years ago, the number of people living in the San Juan Islands increased—at least that is the interpretation of archaeologists based on the large number of shell middens found on the shores of the islands that have deposits laid down during the 1,000–year interval of the Marpole Phase. Presumably more people moved from the river edges, river deltas, and large bays of the mainland to occupy the islands year-round. They not only came to fish during the spring, summer, and fall and to collect berries, dig camas and clams, but they also stayed all winter with these stored goods. These extended visitations on the islands increased the number of sites and the deposits laid down. These people made exquisite carvings, stone tools, and weavings. They excelled in industries and crafts that are now considered traditional for living Northwest Coast peoples. Archaeologists know a great deal about this phase because they have excavated a large number of sites, including the Cattle Point and English Camp sites.

4. The San Juan Phase. The last phase identified by King was found in only a few locations near the present beach (as opposed to the upper beach). He called this the *Late Phase* and thought it represented the time when the bays filled with sediment and the shoreline built outward

This photo, most likely taken in 1948, shows the location of the "lower beach excavation," where King found artifacts he classified as being from the Late Phase. The archaeologists in the left center of the photo are standing in an area filled with sand. When this bay had less sand, waves crashed against the bluff, carving the slopes that are now covered with grass. (Photographer unknown; courtesy of the Burke Museum of Natural History and Culture, Archaeology Archives)

away from the bluff. The beaches, in other words, looked much like they do today. The layers in this phase contain an abundance of shell but fewer artifacts of all kinds than the layers below. According to King, this was a period when people used Cattle Point only sporadically, favoring other, more productive ones elsewhere in the islands.

The phase name used most frequently today is not King's Late Phase but rather the *San Juan Phase* (also called the Gulf of Georgia Culture Type). Sites from this period include triangular projectile points and small numbers of bone objects and woodworking tools. One characteristic of this phase is a decrease in the number of chipped stone tools compared to the Marpole Phase. People did not make as many stone tools, and perhaps they shifted to an even greater dependence on objects made of wood. The San Juan Phase or Late Phase began between 1,500 and 1,100 years ago.

The San Juan Phase is difficult to explain. The archaeological record contains few objects of decoration or art, yet when explorers arrived in the Northwest they observed people with a rich and elaborate artistic repertoire, so rich that collectors scrambled madly to acquire the material. Dependence on wood (and its rapid decomposition in the ground) is one explanation for the changes in stone and bone tool frequencies from the Middle Period (Marpole Phase) to the Late Phase (San Juan Phase). The research conducted at English Camp, however, suggests other explanations, such as the manner in which archaeologists excavate sites and the misuse of radiocarbon dating. Some of the Marpole Phase sites could have been misidentified as being deposited during the San Juan Phase, and San Juan Phase sites as being deposited during the Marpole Phase. The research at English Camp, reported later in this book, obtained radiocarbon dates of almost fifty shell and charcoal samples to explore the reason for the confusion in dating. The research demonstrates clearly that large numbers of radiocarbon ages must be obtained from all the sites excavated. Until this is done we will not know whether the observed changes in technology and subsistence are real or whether they should be considered characteristic of either the Marpole or San Juan Phase.

LIFE AT CATTLE POINT

The native people who lived at Cattle Point obviously performed many activities in their daily lives. The archaeological evidence collected by King, however, tells us about only some of them. Unfortunately, we do not know as much as we could, because King and Burroughs used collection techniques acceptable in 1946 through 1948 but very different from those used today. King screened the dark sandy sediment through quarter-inch mesh. He was interested in separating the large bone and stone tools from the dark matrix that hid them. As much as 99 percent of fish bone falls through a quarter-inch mesh. King was surprised by the fact that he did not find more evidence of fishing (not many fish bones). Perhaps the reason was that he could not see the bone in the dark matrix and his screens were not small enough to catch them.

Moreover, King did not save the shellfish, charcoal, or large rocks he must have encountered. The shellfish were so abundant that he believed that a listing of the species present was adequate to indicate the subsistence practices of the people. He did not save much charcoal because radiocarbon dating was just in the earliest stages of development, and he had not heard of the technique. The little charcoal he saved was for the purpose of identifying wood species used as fuel and for tool manufacture. He also failed to save, or even record, the presence of pebbles or cobbles if they showed no evidence of abrasion or perforation. The numbers of stones used in roasting pits, in the hot-rock boiling technique, or as anchors for posts are therefore not known. In King's defense, the standard archaeological practices in the middle of the twentieth century did not include recording or saving these data.

Shellfishing

The people living in the San Juan Islands at the time of contact with Europeans, the Strait Salish, depended on a variety of marine invertebrates, and evidence from the Cattle Point site indicates that that dependence has existed for the last few thousand years. Members of the Lummi and Songhees tribes told Dr. Wayne Suttles that most gathering occurs either by walking the shoreline at low tide or from a canoe. Cockles, edible mussels, native oysters, and sea cucumbers were picked up from the surface of exposed flats, sometimes pried loose with a digging stick. Chitons, snails, barnacles, and sea urchins were picked off exposed rocks. Clams were dug with a digging stick from either gravel or mud flats. Crabs were picked up by waders or speared from canoes. Open-weave baskets were used to collect the marine invertebrates, allowing the water to drain out the bottom.

Lucy Lane Handeyside (born in 1893), an elder of the Lummi Nation, remembers:

> My mother used to eat sea cucumbers but we didn't like them. Didn't like the looks of them. Too ugly. We also ate a seafood that looked like a little bootie. They were not mussels. They weren't Chinese hats. They stick on rocks. You pry them off. You don't cook them long. You bring them to a boil and take them right off. The shell is black and the meat is pinkish-white. I used to go with my mother and gather them. My mother used to eat sea urchins but I wouldn't. They used to eat them raw. I never did. I couldn't stand the looks of them. Anyway, I want my food cooked. (*Lummi Elders Speak*, p. 50)

Cooking methods for shellfish vary. Suttles's informants report that "rock clams" and cockles were broken and eaten raw, but they

These trenches are the excavations of the Cattle Point site in 1948. The sediment in the upper beach is very sandy, which causes the walls of the excavation units to collapse. Note the boards pressed against the walls of the trenches to prevent collapse. (Photographer unknown; courtesy of the Burke Museum, Archaeology Archives)

could also be steamed (Suttles 1968, pp. 65-66). Mussels were thrown on the fire and roasted or steamed. Butter clams were steamed or, like rock clams and horse clams, they were roasted and dried for winter use. Clams were steamed on a bed of hot rocks in a pit about 2 feet deep and 4 feet across. Cobble-sized rocks were placed on top of sticks and the fire lit. After the rocks got red hot, they were dropped into the ashes, then the ashes were removed, and the base of the pit leveled off. The clams were laid on top of the rocks and covered with kelp blades or white fir boughs. After about fifteen minutes, if the clams had opened, they were taken out and eaten.

Roasting and drying clams required some additional work. Butter clams were steamed first, then roasted and dried to preserve them for winter consumption or for trade. After the shells opened in the steam pit, the meat was removed and washed. Each animal was strung on an ironwood stick and tied. The loaded sticks were leaned against a horizontal pole above a fire. After the clams were roasted and the sticks removed, the clams were threaded together on a cedar bark line. The line was then dried, either at the beach in a roughly built plank shed or at the winter location in a smokehouse. Cockles

This is another view of the 1948 excavations of the Cattle Point site (showing same area as in previous photo). The rectangular wooden frame behind the piles of dirt in the background is a screen. Wire mesh with one-quarter-inch openings was stretched across the frame. All the sediment was sifted through the screen to recover artifacts. Any object smaller than the size of the mesh (e.g., most fish bone) fell through the mesh and was lost. Archaeologists excavating today use smaller-mesh screens, one-eighth inch at the largest. Small fish bones are thus recovered. (Photographer unknown; courtesy of the Burke Museum, Archaeology Archives)

and rock clams were also roasted and strung on lines, but they were not steamed first. The lines of about thirty clams were often traded with people from the plateau (eastern Washington and British Columbia) for smoked fish.

According to Al Charles (born in 1896), an elder of the Lummi Nation:

> In the early part of the preserving season, the people would go out and get clams and they would shell them out there, bring them back in baskets, build a great big fire pit, and cook them. After they were cooked, they'd string them up on cedar strips and hang them up to dry. They preserved from about June right through the winter. Berries started to ripen the latter part of June and July. They had the equipment all ready for the berries. They'd spread that all on top of the roof of a house or on racks

and let the sun dry their berries. Those berries were put away for the winter like the dried clams. (*Lummi Elders Speak,* p. 51)

The Strait Salish people told Suttles that shellfish were gathered at any time. The best time, however, was summer, when the meat tasted better and the clams were easier to dry. These people told Suttles that they also preferred to travel to one favorite clamming location and process large numbers of clams right there, rather than stopping at many locations. Some of the locations were owned by an individual who supervised the collecting, steaming, and drying processes. Everyone helped collect and shell the clams, but women were usually the supervisors and most likely the owners of the shellfish bed. Ownership was handed down through kinship lines and meant entitlement to the resources. Others had to pay for resources. Knowledge about the location and the resource was also owned and handed down only to relatives, so knowledge about the clams, as well as the clams, could be owned.

The shellfish found at Cattle Point are predominantly those kinds that can be roasted and dried for later consumption and trade. In the earliest deposits, mussels dominate the assemblage. The proportion is not known, but King commented on their condition being fragmented and heavily decomposed. He suggests that the lack of other shellfish may have been the result of unfavorable preservation conditions. Mussels, however, are one of the first kinds of shells to decompose, because they have such thin shells. If King found mussel shells in the lowest deposits of the Developmental Phase, then mussels were probably the primary shellfish collected at that time. Mussels appear first in some sites close to the Fraser River delta (e.g., the Crescent Beach site, at the town of Crescent Beach, British Columbia) and may be the first shellfish collected in Puget Sound as well (they were found at the West Point Site in Seattle).

In deposits laid down during the Maritime Phase King found (in decreasing order of abundance) horse clam, venus clam, cockle, bentnose clam, mussels, scallops, oysters, and snails of various kinds, including large whelks; he postulated that Cattle Point became a place where shellfish were collected and processed in large numbers. The season of that occupation and activity was most likely early to late summer, perhaps during and after the salmon fishing season.

Reef-netting Salmon

Although King did not find many fish bones at the Cattle Point site, the configuration of the landscape and artifacts found in the Maritime and Late Phase deposits suggest that Cattle Point may have been a superb location for catching salmon. It was probably an excellent location for catching all kinds of fish, but today salmon are caught by the numerous fishermen who troll in front of the site.

Catching salmon in the open ocean is far more difficult than catching them in a confined river with waterfalls, shallow rapids, and bedrock constrictions. The technique in use today is reef-netting. Its age is unknown. The archaeologist Diane Hanson suggests that reef-netting was invented very recently, close to the time of contact with Europeans. She bases this interpretation on the relative abundance of salmon bones in archaeological deposits of various ages compared to the bones of other fish species. Only in the most recent deposits does the amount of salmon increase significantly over that of other fish.

Native Americans today know from their traditions that reef-netting is ancient. Huge numbers of fish bones are recovered from Northwest Coast sites, yet until recently most were not analyzed. They were ignored because so vast are their numbers that it is difficult and expensive to identify and interpret them. More analysis of fish bones, as in Hanson's study, is being completed every year to sort out this issue.

At Cattle Point, King did not systematically save fish bones but rather noted their presence as he excavated and saved those that remained in the large screen. No one knows the method of catching fish used at Cattle Point or if reef-netting was important at this location. Many features found at the Cattle Point site suggest that fish processing was a major activity there. I will describe the reef-netting technique and the features found at the Cattle Point site and let readers draw their own conclusions.

According to Suttles's informants, reef-netting was a method of catching migrating salmon before they reached the rivers in which they spawned. An artificial reef was constructed using two canoes, a net stretched between the canoes, and an elaborate system of anchors, buoys, and cooperative labor. The system required many people and newly manufactured equipment. In past times, men worked the canoes and nets, while women processed the fish on shore. A reef-net location and gear were owned by an individual, and the crew was led by a captain (sometimes the owner was the captain).

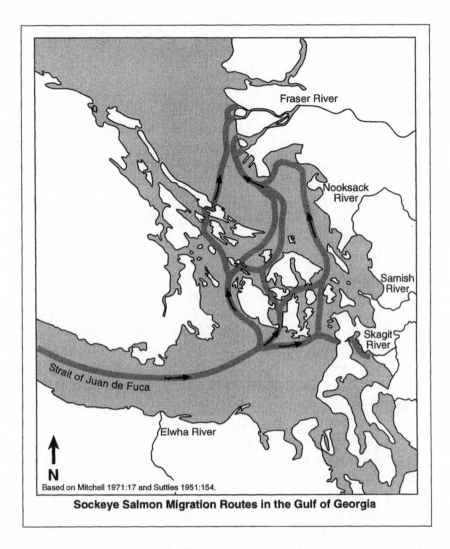

Sockeye Salmon Migration Routes in the Gulf of Georgia

Sockeye salmon spend their adult lives in the open ocean. Their last act is to spawn after a long voyage back to the river of their birth. Most of the sockeye born in the Fraser River return from the ocean along a pathway through the San Juan islands. Salmon do not eat during this return voyage; rather, they rely on the fat stored in their body to sustain them. The closer to the ocean a fish is caught, the greater its fat content; thus, sockeye caught within the San Juan islands have more fat than those taken from the Fraser River.

Al Charles (born in 1896), an elder of the Lummi Nation, reports:

And they had shelters where they made their equipment, like lumber, rope, fishing equipment. Near where they built their canoes, their mutual fishing location was well known. Each family had their reef

These canoes are part of a complex reef-netting setup. Fish swim from left to right, into each V-shaped net arrangement. Men in the canoes are watching for fish to arrive. (Photograph by Wayne and Shirley Suttles, 1949; courtesy of the Burke Museum, neg. 1017-C)

netting location. Each location had a name. It dates way back. They just didn't go and step on somebody's toes. They were trained in those days how to put up their dwellings, their great big buildings, and how to make their fishing equipment, hunting equipment and build their canoes. They were the best canoe builders, well-trained. They would have a good supply of canoes so they could trade and sell to people who wanted to pay. (*Lummi Elders Speak,* p. 66)

Slaves were especially important to the owners and participants of fishing locations. Slaves were usually war captives and significant as trade items. Leland Donald describes slaves as personal attendants and even sacrificial victims for the Nootka of Vancouver Island and important as additional labor. Reef-netting was so productive that personal slaves were put to work processing fish. Only in this way could all the fish be cleaned, dried, and stored before they spoiled.

Reef-netting is still practiced today along the migration routes of fish in many parts of the San Juan and Gulf islands and along the mainland coast. Presumably it was practiced in these same locations in the past. The fish return from feeding in the open ocean and follow various routes through the islands on their way to spawning grounds up the

Herman Olsen (born in 1909), an elder of the Lummi Nation, describes reef-netting in the early 19th century: "When we went out there and put in those reef nets, we caught fish right off starting the first day and the white fishermen never had one to eat. They didn't know how to catch them. They didn't know how to use a reef net. Every night when we'd go home, you could go down and sit on the beach and see them out there measuring our reef net and copying it. They'd wait until it was nighttime before they'd go and copy our reef net. Measure all the lines and then they'd go back and try to fix theirs the same way" (Lummi Elders Speak, p. 26). (Photograph from Special Collections and Preservation Division, University of Washington Libraries, neg. NA 1810)

Fraser River. All the reef-netting locations remembered by tribal elders were along these migration routes.

The best reef-netting locations were usually short distances from shore on kelp-covered reefs that lay in the path of migrating sockeye salmon. Such locations had to have appropriate currents, clear water, and adequate beaches nearby for the placement of the summer camp and processing site.

In such locations the kelp was cleared away to make a channel for the fish to follow into the waiting net. If there was no kelp or the water was deep, then an artificial channel was made by hanging kelp on the side lines and bottom net lines to trick the fish. Huge anchor stones, lifted by as many as four men, held the nets in place, and buoys kept the lines accessible and the net in the proper place.

This shed-roof building with baskets was photographed at the Lummi Nation sometime between 1930 and 1933. The mats forming the walls at the rear of the shed were made of either cattails or tules. Aurelia Balch Celestine (born in 1886), an elder of the Lummi Nation, describes making these mats: "They used the cattail to make mats out of. They made several and used them for their mattress. And whenever they'd go any place, like camping out, they'd take mats along and use them for their shelter. They used the cattail for the roof because it doesn't leak. The tules they used that for the sides. Tules soak easily so they don't use them for the roof. They'd gather them and they'd dry them. They'd make long needles out of hardwood. Oh, the needles must have been about three feet. Some of them are long and some of them are short. But the longer it is, the better, I guess. They used the finer parts from the cattail and they put that together and they twisted it. They made string out of that and they used that to put those tules together. They didn't use strings. If they used strings, it would cut, you know. It's a lot of work" (Lummi Elders Speak, p. 46). *(Photograph by Eugene Field; Special Collections and Preservation Division, University of Washington Libraries, neg. NA 1848)*

Specific current conditions were necessary. Most currents change direction with the ebb and flow of the tide, yet fish swim only toward the river. If the currents in a location ran too swiftly, then the net would rise to the surface; if the current ran against the net, then the anchors could dislodge. The net could be used only on ebb or flow tides and only in locations where the currents were not too strong.

The water had to be clear enough for the captain to see the fish swim into the net. At his signal, the canoes were released from their anchors and pulled together by the weight of the net. The fish in the net

This shed with mat walls and roof was photographed by Edward S. Curtis in 1912 at the Skokomish fishing camp. Curtis was famous for "setting up" his photos, sometimes requiring his subjects to stand for hours while he adjusted lighting and his camera. (Courtesy of the Burke Museum)

were dumped into one canoe as the net was drawn into the other. The fish were transported to shore in one of two ways. When one of the two canoes was full, then either a third canoe was rowed from shore by the women to replace the full one or the canoe with the fish was detached from the net and the occupants paddled to shore and dumped the fish.

Traditionally the summer camp and processing site were set up in a systematic arrangement. The owner's house (sometimes made of planks for the roof and mats for the walls) was set back from the shore and faced the water. In front of this house were many fish-drying racks. Adjacent to the racks were trenches in which fires were sometimes built to help dry the fish or to add smoke. Around the drying racks, beyond the trenches, were the houses of the crew. These houses were usually made of poles with mats as roofs and walls. Mats sometimes were laid on the floor as well. The fish were processed on the beach in front of the drying racks.

Fish were traditionally processed in much the same way all over the Northern Straits area. Each fish was cut to remove the head, spine, and

This photo of a Makah woman tending fish drying on racks was taken between 1890 and 1900 at Neah Bay. The Makah people do not speak the Coast Salish language and are not considered Strait Salish. Nonetheless, their fish-processing practices are similar to those of people in the islands, and so these images are included in this book. The fish on these racks are hung both along their backbone and across their middle, as described by Herman Olsen (born in 1909), an elder of the Lummi Nation: "They catch lingcod and split them in half. Take each half right off the backbone. You take that backbone right out and throw it away. And you take a pole and hang one half of one on one side and other half you hang on the other side so the backs aren't touching together. That's the way you hang them up to dry. They hang them up single too. They bust that up and make soup, the belly part. They take salmon and split it like you were going to hang it up to smoke, and you smoke it about a day and half or two days and you take it down and cut it right in half down the middle, split it again. Then you hang it up to where it'll really be as dry as a board" (Lummi Elders Speak, p. 57) (Photograph by Samuel Morse; Special Collections and Preservation Division, University of Washington Libraries, neg. NA 715)

tail as one piece, leaving two halves of meat, sometimes spread open and held that way by two wooden splints. Fish were then hung on the drying racks. The bones of the fish were, therefore, left at the camp, with only the flesh and skin dried and transported to a winter village location. Suttles reports that some women left the backbone and fins on the fish, and there are some photographs of drying fish with heads attached. But most descriptions of cutting fish suggest that the head, vertebrae, and tail were left together. Some descriptions suggest that these skeleton parts were also dried and stored for the winter to be used to flavor stews or soups.

This woman is tending fish and clams drying on racks. The clams are strung together and draped along the first rack. The fish are on the rear rack. Note that the fish are covered with a mat against rain or too much sun. Photo taken on beach near Port Townsend between 1895 and 1900. (Photograph by W. H. Wilcox; Special Collections and Preservation Division, University of Washington Libraries, neg. NA 840)

The fish skeletons and organs left at the camp may have been cleaned up at the end of the fishing season. According to Diamond Jenness, an observer of the Saanich people,

This photo taken around 1898 depicts the vast network of fish-drying racks at Tatoosh Island (a Makah village). Some fish are hanging along their backbones (top of the rear rack), most along their middle. Note the smokehouse in the front of the photo. (Photograph by Samuel Morse; Special Collections and Preservation Division, University of Washington Libraries, neg. NA 716)

> Women and children, under the supervision of the priest, gathered up all the loose sticks and refuse on the beach and piled them in a heap. Then towards midnight everyone rose, lit the bonfire, and threw into the air balls of mixed deer-fat, camas, and bird's down, yelling the names of the places they fished and saying "I feed you this." Then they scattered their fire, threw the burning brands in play at one another, and yelled and danced until daylight, when they packed up their belongings and returned to the Saanich Peninsula. (Jenness 1934, p. 21)

Jenness may be describing a process whereby camp refuse, including fish bones, was gathered into piles and burned to ash on the beach, explaining why at some sites thick lenses of burned bone, shell, and ash are found.

Evidence of reef-netting at the Cattle Point site is scanty but suggestive. The salmon migrate in front of the beach today, and according to elders they did so in the past as well. A ledge, or reef, extends outward from the shore and causes the fish to rise toward the surface. The currents are appropriately strong, and they shift as the tide ebbs and flows. Archaeologists have looked underwater on the reef for evi-

This trench contains a long linear arrangement of stones. Clay ridges in the middle connect some of the stones. The hearths and postholes are in the far end. Note that to the right and left of the trench far fewer stones were found, just more sand with some artifacts. The stones were put in these positions by the people occupying Cattle Point. Whether they were placed in this arrangement all at once or added over many years is not known. (Photographer unknown; courtesy of the Burke Museum, Archaeology Archives)

A close-up of some of the stones in the trench demonstrates that they do not outline hearth pits or form any discernible pattern. One hypothesis is that they stabilized in the sandy substrate the poles used to support drying racks. (Photographer unknown; courtesy of the Burke Museum, Archaeology Archives)

dence of anchor stones (large boulders that held nets in place and kept canoes apart). Nothing was found, but it is possible that such stones were buried below layers of sediment accumulated at the shoreline in recent years.

A mysterious stone alignment was discovered during King's 1947 excavation. A long trench, dug by the occupants of the site, was found with rocks and clay features scattered throughout. King believed that the trench dates from the Developmental Phase because it contained artifacts he associated with that time period. In 1948 Burroughs reopened the trench and continued his excavation to determine the origin and function of the trench and to find any additional stone and clay features. From these two excavations we know that the trench was 67 feet long and contained stone slab structures connected by clay ridges. The stone arrangements were rectangular, square, and circular and composed of large slabs of schist and gneiss. None of them had tops or bottoms, only walls of stone slabs. Running through and connecting the slabs were ridges of hard-packed, light-colored clay. One of these ridges was 15 feet long and .5 feet wide. Connected to it was a clay-lined fire pit containing charcoal and ash. The clay ran through the center of all the stone structures and had to have been brought to the trench by the original inhabitants and laid carefully on the sand and between the stones. According to King, the clay may have served as the floor of the stone structures.

Also found in the trench were postholes and hearths. Postholes are places where small posts had been shoved into the ground but later rotted away, leaving a dark stain. Hearths are features with abundant charcoal and rocks cracked by heat. They are usually circular and sometimes lined with clay or rocks. King found a lens-shaped hearth and concentrations of charcoal that he was confident were fire pits.

Perhaps the most unusual features found near the trench were clay "bowls." King thought these bowls were younger than the trench, from the Maritime Phase, yet they were closely associated with the stones. None of the charcoal (or the bowls themselves) were saved, so we cannot test this hypothesis. King found three bowl-shaped clay features, each over a foot in diameter and seemingly molded together at the time of manufacture. The bowls were constructed by first digging a pit into the sand, then placing slabs of stone and small beach cobbles within the pits. Finally, the walls were cemented in place with clay. One of the three bowls had only clay to form the walls, no stones. One interpretation is that the circular clay bowls might have

Six circular bowl-shaped features were found at the Cattle Point site. During the 1947 excavation, the group of three bowls whose sides were touching (shown above) was found. All bowls were made by mixing clay with sand and cobbles, then hardened by firing. The bowls above had reddish stains on their inner surfaces, with remnants of charcoal, fish vertebrae, and shell. The single bowl (shown below) displayed no reddish evidence of burning or any charcoal, shell, or bone. King rejects the idea that the bowls were used for cooking, because their porosity was too great and little evidence of fire was found near them. (Photographer unknown; courtesy of the Burke Museum, Archaeology Archives)

been associated with cooking, because they contained charcoal, fish vertebrae, and shell and displayed a reddish color on the inside surface, interpreted as the result of burning. The clay bowls rested on top of a 1-inch "floor" of clay measuring 8 feet by 4. Burroughs found two additional bowls in 1948, neither of which had anything inside nor reddish surfaces.

Similar clay bowl features were found at one other site in the region, the Pitt River site on the Lower Fraser River. The bowls were thought to be for processing roots. King excavated the surrounding sediment away from the "bowls," but they were more likely made and used as clay-lined depressions within the surrounding sediment in which something was poured, stored, or roasted. Finding the bowl features at Pitt River and Cattle Point suggests they were an invention used by many people in the region.

Perhaps the trench, stone boxes, clay features, and the circular clay bowl structures were used for fish processing. The dimensions and placement of the trench match descriptions made by elders and recorded by Suttles of a summer reef-netting camp. At such places trenches were dug to hold posts for the fish-drying racks. Inside the trenches were laid fires to help dry the hanging fish and deter insects from laying eggs on the meat. The stone and clay structures in the trench are not described in these accounts, but they may be similar to constructs used more recently. The stones and clay may have acted as anchors for drying-rack supports or for house posts. The age of this stone structure is unknown, but it may have been laid down as many as 3,500 to 2,500 years ago. Ethnographic analogies may not be appropriate for such an ancient feature, and Suttles's informants apparently had no recollections that bear directly on the stones or bowls.

There is some evidence to support the idea that the trenches were used to dry fish. The substrate at Cattle Point is sand and gravel, a very unstable surface for construction. It would be difficult to keep a post vertical in this substrate. The clay or stones found in the trenches could have helped keep such a post in place. Although the location is ideal for drying, because the wind blows day and night off the Strait of Juan de Fuca from the southwest, the wind could have blown down any structure with foundation posts that were not weighted and anchored into the ground. Archaeologists found four perforated anchor stones in this trench, along with some net weights. Besides functioning as an anchor, the clay ridge may have held down a wall made of mats. The clay floor may have protected a processing area from the sand below it.

Archaeologists call large perforated ground stones anchor stones. These are four of the thirteen anchor stones found at the Cattle Point site, some with incomplete perforations, some elliptical, and others rectangular. Stones were most likely used to anchor either nets in water or poles used in drying. (Photograph by Nancy Morningstar)

Another interpretation is that the trench, stones, and hearths are related to a house structure. Evidence of houses at Cattle Point has been particularly elusive. King reported that "on the surface of the site, and as revealed in profiles, there is evidence to show that the inhabitants of the site utilized depressions as living quarters during their stay at Cattle Point" (King, p. 73). King believed that some of these depressions were blow-outs, (holes created by the wind when vegetation is removed from the surface), and others were purposely created by piling refuse in circular ridges. Temporary shelters could have been erected over these depressions, but no evidence of such shelters has been found. Perhaps someone excavated a trench next to, or associated with, a house structure, and the stones, hearths, clay ridges, and clay bowls are connected to some activity that is no longer practiced by Native Americans.

Evidence of the houses made in the Northwest before contact comes mostly from informants and historical descriptions. These pre-

This large anchor stone was found among the other rocks in the trench. Its presence suggests the need to weigh down materials at the site, both nets used for fishing and racks used for drying. (Photographer unknown; courtesy of the Burke Museum, Archaeology Archives)

contact structures were rectangular and made of cedar planks, called plank houses. The dwellings people built 3,500 to 2,500 years ago may have been very different from the plank houses built 500 years ago. An excavation outside Sequim has uncovered a structure made within a depression, roughly the same age as the depressions at Cattle Point. Finding evidence of such dwellings in the Northwest is unusual, however, similar structures were built for thousands of years east of the Cascade range in the plateau region, especially along the Columbia and Fraser Rivers.

Houses built in depressions, called pithouses, are ingenious structures for survival in the very cold, snowy climate of the plateau. In 1997,

Vera Morgan from Eastern Washington University uncovered near the town of Sequim a depression with rock features that are in some ways similar to those found at the Cattle Point site. She believes that the Sequim depression (especially with its sides excavated into the landscape, the pattern of postholes, and the location of its central hearth) is very similar to plateau pithouses. It differs in that its outline is roughly rectangular. It is about 2,300 years old. The Sequim site had no baked clay ridges or bowls like those found at the Cattle Point site.

Perhaps King discovered house depressions similar to the pithouses found at Sequim or along the Fraser River but did not recognize them as such. After all, he was expecting to find plank houses similar to those made by people living recently on the Northwest Coast, not pithouse depressions similar to those made by people living in the plateau. King believed that the traditions of the people living on the coast extended far back in time. He suggested that, as more native people were interviewed, information about erecting shelters in depressions would be found. The opposite seems to have occurred. The archaeological record seems to suggest that people may have first built houses closer in style to those found in the plateau region, and only later did they build the plank houses characteristic of Northwest Coast cultures.

The features found at Cattle Point provide an excellent example of how archaeologists interpret the past. The most important observations associated with the trench were not the individual objects found there but rather their spatial and contextual relationships. Context is defined by archaeologists as the three-dimensional association of objects in space and time. We determine context by using systematic extraction methods; for example, we dig square holes with ninety-degree corners and then measure every object's and layer's depth below a set elevation point. We also screen all the sediment extracted, keeping track of the objects that are found together in the same layer, and the objects' stratigraphic arrangement (placement above and below one other). All these methods were developed over decades of archaeological advancement, and they all refine our ability to record the context of objects.

Today, we may not be able to satisfy all of our curiosity about the activity that produced the trench, hearths, and clay bowls. King offered one explanation. Now, with new information from other excavations in nearby areas, we can offer another explanation. The contexts of the objects have been carefully recorded, so our findings can be used by scholars for centuries to come. No doubt those future scholars will invent entirely new interpretations based on these data, and we may

King excavated the trench containing the concentrations of stones and the clay ridges in 1946 and 1947. This photo of that trench, taken in 1948 before Burroughs began his excavation, indicates that King did not backfill his trench and that the wind at Cattle Point made short work of collapsing the walls and filling the hole. Note also that ferns already cover the piles of dirt adjacent to the trench. (Photographer unknown; courtesy of the Burke Museum, Archaeology Archives)

never be able to determine the relevance of these unusual features. They remind us, however, that the past may have been very different from the present and, therefore, that context is vital within archaeology.

Few of the artifacts found at Cattle Point support or weaken the hypothesis that this location was the site of a reef-netting camp or a pit-house. One in particular, however, sharpens the focus of the picture we are trying to reconstruct. This lovely object is a whale-bone spindle whorl, used for processing fiber for weaving. Many carved spindle whorls collected from Coast Salish people are found in museum collections; however, most of them are made of wood. This bone spindle

45-SJ-1

This is the only spindle whorl found at the Cattle Point site, and it was discovered in the layers near the top, believed to date from the Maritime Phase. Spindle whorls made of wood are frequently used by Northwest Coast women for spinning. Bone spindle whorls like this one are less common. (Photograph by Nancy Morningstar)

whorl is not decorated, but its presence indicates that the technology of spinning fibers is ancient in the region. As for what fiber was being spun, and for what purpose, no one can say. Mountain goat wool and the wool from small domesticated dogs were valued by Northwest Coast weavers before cloth was introduced from Europe. Whatever the fiber, the presence of the whorl at Cattle Point indicates that weavers were busily making either nets, fishing lines, or warm robes for members of a canoe crew.

CONCLUSIONS

The Cattle Point shell midden, protected within the boundaries of American Camp at San Juan Island National Historical Park, has provided archaeologists with fascinating information about the people who

This Cowichan woman demonstrates the appropriate way to use a spindle whorl to make yarn. (Photographer unknown; courtesy of the Burke Museum)

lived in the San Juan Islands for thousands of years. King thought that the location was originally used as a permanent residence throughout the year, shifting to a seasonal residence relatively recently. He believed that the first people here depended only on resources that came from the land, and none from the sea. These people left artifacts and mammal remains but did not leave remains of shellfish, fish, or marine mammals. Later people began collecting marine resources, first mussels and fish, followed by all available shellfish, fish, marine mammals, and land mammals. According to King, these marine-adapted people built houses in depressions, constructed a trench with stone-slab boxes connected by clay ridges, and made clay bowls that were somehow related to their subsistence.

Most of King's interpretations still stand today and have been corroborated by excavations on Lopez, Orcas, Sucia, and Decatur islands. For example, other sites contain evidence that 2,500 years ago a large number of people came to the islands and started depending on marine resources to a much greater extent than they had previously. Most sites in the San Juan Islands are shell middens that date from within the last

1,500 years. King identified a rare occupation of the earliest people in the San Juan Islands at Cattle Point. The initial occupation was small and covered with the material dropped by later people.

Some of King's conclusions we now know to be mistaken. Cattle Point was probably never a place where people built permanent homes and lived throughout the year. The exposed windy slope observed today was most likely the landscape since the end of the Ice Age. Dr. James Agee, a forester at the University of Washington, analyzed all the evidence relevant to the question of whether the south shore of American Camp was ever forested; he suggests that no trees covered the area at any time in the past. The substrate is too sandy, the wind too fierce for a large forest to develop on this south-facing slope, and the rainfall is too low in the rain shadow of the Olympics. Without a forest to provide some protection from the wind, Cattle Point would not make an attractive wintering location.

With the information from this site and others that continue to be excavated, as well as that from Native Americans alive today, most scholars theorize that the Cattle Point location was a summer camp throughout its occupation, a place where people came together to collect and process food. The slopes facing the Strait of Juan de Fuca are just too windy to provide adequate protection for people living here in the winter, even if they lived in a pithouse rather than a plank house. Many locations in the San Juan Islands were likely occupied only during the summer over the last 5,000 years and especially during the last 2,500 years. These summer places were most likely for the primary purpose of hunting, fishing, and processing.

Since King's and Burroughs's research, no further excavations have been conducted at Cattle Point. In 1990 the backdirt (sediment originally removed by King but used to refill the excavated holes) from one of King's excavations was screened by students from the University of Washington field school (students were excavating at English Camp). Lots of small stone chips (byproducts of stone point manufacturing) and fish bones were recovered. No charcoal was found. Other areas could be excavated to extract the small fish bones, charcoal, and stratigraphic information that modern archaeologists now collect. This project has been proposed to the National Park Service and awaits funding and consultation with the Native Americans.

This photo shows the view to the south of the Strait of Juan de Fuca as seen from the upper bank at the Cattle Point site. Note the fishing boats poised above the offshore reef and the driftwood on the shore. One of King's excavation units is visible in the lower portion of the photo. (Photographer unknown, 1948; courtesy of the Burke Museum, Archaeology Archives)

In 1948 historic buildings were still present near the fresh-water spring. Note archaeologists taking a lunch break near the car on the left. (Photographer unknown; courtesy of the Burke Museum, Archaeology Archives)

ENGLISH CAMP SITE

The English Camp site (45SJ24) is located on the eastern shore of Garrison Bay in a protected inlet. Unlike Cattle Point, English Camp is remembered by Native Americans as a winter village. The archaeological evidence in the San Juan Islands suggests that people first came to the islands for summer food, and only later stayed in the islands over the winter. Excavations at English Camp revealed an interesting first step in that transition. The first winter houses may have been very different from the houses people today remember.

The archaeological shell midden underlies the grassy open area of the park (called the Parade Grounds) and the wooded region to the north. The National Park Service maintains the grassy area to replicate the landscape as it appeared during the British occupation from 1860 to 1872. Before the British occupation, when the site was inhabited by Native Americans, the area was mostly forested, and a brackish-water wetland covered the low-lying (northeastern) part of the Parade Grounds. We know where the Native Americans occupied the landscape because they dropped shell, animal bones, and artifacts over a broad area. The artifacts from the prehistoric occupations extend for several hundred meters along the shores of the bay and around the wetlands. The British occupation was predominantly restricted to the Parade Grounds and the Officers Quarters on the bedrock hill to the south.

The largest English Camp excavations (referred to by Stein as Operations) occurred in two areas: the Parade Grounds (Operation A) and the wooded area to the north (Operation D). The deposits in the

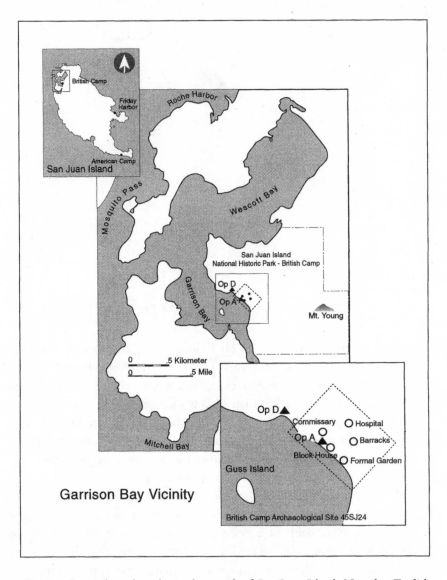

Garrison Bay is located on the northwest side of San Juan Island. Note that English Camp is on Garrison Bay, with Wescott Bay just to the north and Mitchell Bay to the south. Houses associated with prehistoric winter villages might have been located in both Garrison and Mitchell bays.

Parade Grounds have been affected by many people over the years: landscaping done by Native Americans and British soldiers; farming by the Crook family, who homesteaded the land after the British left; and development and restoration of the site by the National Park Service, who built facilities to improve visitor accessibility. The wooded area has been affected less. Trees were cleared in the 1940s, and some shell was removed by the British and William Crook, to be used as construction fill and for paving pathways. We must keep in mind all of these alterations as we imagine the landscape as the Native Americans encountered and used it.

THE AGE OF THE
ENGLISH CAMP SHELL MIDDEN

The age of occupations at English Camp has been measured using radiocarbon dating. Stein collected and analyzed samples from the excavations in both Operation D (the wooded area) and Operation A (the unit in the Parade Grounds). The dating indicates that people first lived in the wooded area, but only for a short time. Then they lived in the flat area of the Parade Grounds until the British soldiers and American settlers arrived.

The oldest sample in the wooded area of the site Operation D dates from approximately A.D. 100. Analysis of twenty-four other samples from this area reveals that most of the material accumulated over a relatively short period of time from A.D. 500 to A.D. 800. These ages were unexpected—Stein had believed that the shell midden in the northern wooded area was deposited over a long period of time, from A.D. 100 to A.D. 1800. We now know that the shell midden was built quickly, used, and abandoned all within a few hundred years around A.D. 600.

The oldest sample obtained from the shell midden in the Parade Grounds (excavated by Stein in Operation A) dates from approximately A.D. 500. Unlike those from Operation D, however, the majority of these twenty-one samples were less than a thousand years old and ranged over the entire period from A.D. 500 to A.D. 1800. The shell midden in the Parade Grounds was deposited by people over a 1,000-year period (contrasting with the midden in Operation D that accumulated quickly and earlier).

The English Camp site as a whole can be fit within the phase chronology of the southern Northwest Coast. The occupation at English Camp falls near the end of King's Developmental Phase and continues throughout the Maritime and Late Phases. This period corresponds to the Marpole and San Juan Phases. The same people who were fishing and collecting clams at American Camp could have occupied a winter village at English Camp.

The English Camp midden is chronologically similar to many other sites in the region, only a few of which have radiocarbon dates associated with them. English Camp's location on a quiet, protected bay is similar that of a Fossil Bay site on Sucia Island (45SJ105), excavated by Robert Kidd in 1960, and dated by one sample of charcoal as 1,500 years old (A.D. 500).

The Montague Harbour site (DfRu13) on Galiano Island in British Columbia, excavated by Donald Mitchell in 1964 and 1965, is on a protected bay and has features similar to those of English Camp. Montague Harbour contains deposits that are the same age as English Camp's, and it also contains earlier deposits similar in age to those at the Cattle Point site. Charcoal samples that overlap Cattle Point's occupation are 3,200 years and 2,900 years old (1200 B.C. and 900 B.C.). Newer deposits dated from 800 years ago (A.D. 1300) overlap the occupation of English Camp.

On Stuart Island, the Reid Harbor site (45SJ84), excavated in 1977 by Jerry Bailey, contained two dated pieces of charcoal with ages of 2,500 and 2,800 years. On Lopez Island, the Spencer Spit State Park site (45SJ274), excavated in 1980 by James R. Benson, revealed charcoal from 280 and 2,800 years ago, indicating either a long occupation or repeated visits to the same location.

The problem with comparing English Camp with all of these sites is that only at English Camp has an adequate number of samples been subjected to radiocarbon analysis. One or two dates cannot reveal the rates of deposition of shell middens as large as one or two football fields. Forty-five samples were analyzed at English Camp, allowing an interpretation of the approximate age of the excavated portion of the site. Other sites have had only one or two samples dated, thus providing only a tantalizing idea of how long the site might have been occupied.

Other sites in the San Juan Islands that contain artifacts similar to those at English Camp, but that have not been dated radiometrically, include Jeykells Lagoon site (45SJ03) named after George Jakle but spelled incorrectly when recorded in 1946 by Arden King's students; Richardson site (45SJ185), excavated in 1949 by Liston Forbes; Watmough Bight (45SJ280) on Lopez Island, excavated by Robert Greengo and David Munsell in 1968; and the Bonneville Cable Crossing site (45SJ169) on Decatur Island, excavated by R. L. Logsdon in 1975. The similarity of artifacts found in these sites is used to assign these locations to the Marpole and San Juan Phases, indicating that they are comparable in age to the English Camp site. Obviously such comparisons are problematic and can be tested only by submitting multiple samples from

Most of the points found at English Camp are triangular or have small stems (indicating that they were made in the Marpole or San Juan Phases). The majority of these points are also made of a dark rock called dacite (most people would call it basalt). The source of the rock is probably located just north of the Fraser River in a lava flow extruded only about 10,000 years ago, after the glaciers had already melted. This flow is being undercut by the sea. Cobbles of this dacite are rolled by the surf and can be picked up easily by people in a canoe. The rock was transported by people all over the Strait of Georgia, Strait of Juan de Fuca, and (to a lesser extent) Puget Sound. The three points at lower right are made of rock (most likely chert) that is not found in the region but is abundant on the other side of the Cascade Mountains, in eastern Washington and British Columbia. The presence of these chert points at English Camp suggests trade with people living across the Cascades. The people living at English Camp may not have done the trading themselves but rather acquired the material from people living nearer to the mountains, who in turn went over the mountains to trade. (Photograph by Nancy Morningstar)

each site for radiometric analysis. Such a test is now being conducted by Stein using samples from the collections stored at the Burke Museum.

The English Camp site seems to represent occupation of people over the last 2,000 years. The wooded part of the site (Operation D) was occupied for the most part around A.D. 600, sometime at the end of the Marpole Phase and at the beginning of the San Juan Phase. The area under the Parade Grounds (Operation A) was occupied for the most part from A.D. 1000 to the present, mostly within the San Juan Phase.

LIFE AT ENGLISH CAMP

The site designated as English Camp is composed of many landforms and concentrations of Native American and British activities. Excavations in the Parade Grounds revealed a deep, highly stratified shell midden with complex layers of whole and broken shells, rock, charcoal, animal bones, and stone and bone tools. The wooded area, by contrast, revealed a shell midden similar to the one at the Parade Grounds, but on top of which is a ridge of shell midden arranged in a horseshoe shape around a central flat area. The whole structure is about 30 feet wide and 45 feet long, the size of a cabin. The open end of the horseshoe faces Garrison Bay, the rear abuts against the hill. This horseshoe-shaped ridge has been interpreted as the remains of a house, with the structure built in the middle of the horseshoe and the ridge deposited along the outside of three of the walls. After the walls of such a house decayed, the midden piled around the exterior would slump into the middle, creating a horseshoe-shaped feature on the landscape.

The horseshoe ridge is constructed totally of shell midden. The shell in the ridge differs from that in the lower shell midden. It is more frequently burned, crushed, and mixed with ash. Charcoal and organic-rich sediments are less abundant, giving almost half of the shell midden in the ridge a light tan color and chalky feel. Artifacts are found in fewer numbers in the deposits of the ridge, although animal bones and lenses of whole shells are scattered throughout. The origin of the ridge was the focus of Stein's excavations in Operation D.

Most archaeologists agree that since at least A.D. 1500 English Camp was the location of a winter village with plank houses, and most agree that the shell ridge delineates an area that used to be a house. However, the relationship of the shell ridge built around A.D. 600 to the winter occupations dating to A.D. 1500 is not quite so clear. English Camp, especially the Parade Grounds, has the thick accumulations of shell middens that one would expect for a location occupied all winter. Ridges, however, are found only in the wooded area known to be older than the Parade Grounds. Saanich elders reported in the middle of this century that Garrison Bay was the location of a winter village with houses. Pits, hearths, and artifacts found in the Parade Grounds suggest that people's activities at English Camp were typical for winter villages since A.D. 1500. Most convincing is that British soldiers reported dismantling an Indian "longhouse" standing in the Parade Grounds in A.D. 1860; a longhouse (another word meaning plank house) points to winter occupation.

The horseshoe-shaped shell ridge found in the wooded area, however, is not in the location identified as the winter village, looks different from any feature seen or remembered for recent winter villages, and was built and abandoned more than a thousand years before the winter villages were seen by explorers or evidence of traditional plank houses was found in the archaeological record. If it is the remains of a house, then one wonders what kind of house it was, and whether the practice of aggregating into large winter villages was the life-style at A.D. 600.

The horseshoe-shaped ridge at English Camp is not the only one in the area. About ten such ridges were described at the Beach Grove site (DgRs1) just north of Point Roberts, Washington, and south of Tsawwassen, British Columbia. Ten radiocarbon samples suggest that the age of these Beach Grove ridges is similar to that of the ridge at English Camp (between A.D. 300 and 600). Excavations at English Camp (in Operation D) and Beach Grove suggest that such ridges surrounded an early kind of house built in the islands. We do not know if they represent year-round occupation or what kind of superstructure was built within them. In fact, the suggestion that they are a house is really a hypothesis that is still being tested. Data collected thus far suggests that there was a dwelling of some kind. The exact nature of this structure is not yet clear.

Winter Villages

Northwest Coast houses cannot be discussed in terms of single dwellings because they rarely existed on the landscape in isolation but, rather, were part of larger villages. Winter villages were places where many dwellings were built, where people stayed throughout the cold and wet months and returned over a period of many years until a new location was chosen. The groups living in a village were organized around kinship ties. Wayne Suttles describes the organization of a winter village:

> At the time of White settlement the whole area formed a social continuum within which the village was only one of several equally important social groupings. On the basis of winter residence, we might distinguish four levels of discrete units:
>
> *families,* each occupying its own section of a cedar-plank house and maintaining its own domestic economy;
>
> *house groups,* each composed of several families (related through either males or females) occupying a plank house and cooperating as hosts of feasts and other ceremonies;

villages, each composed of a group of such houses occupying a short stretch of beach or river bank and sharing a common name and identification with territory;

tribes, generally composed of several villages occupying a longer stretch of shoreline or a drainage area and sharing a common name and, to some extent, forms of speech, subsistence methods, and ceremonial procedures. (Suttles, *Coast Salish Essays,* p. 210)

House groups seemed to be the strongest social units, through which prestige, wealth, and feuds were maintained. Villages acted together if threatened, but reverted back to house groups as soon as the threat passed.

Garrison Bay has been identified by Lummi people as the location of one winter village. Al Charles (an elder of the Lummi Nation) lists many of the locations of former villages.

Our people had shelters in large buildings not just the small ones. There were big buildings around San Juan Island, Orcas Island, Lopez Island, Point Roberts, Birch Bay, Lummi Bay, Ferndale, Marietta, Fort Bellingham, Whatcom Creek, Chuckanut, Gooseberry Point, Samish Island, and Point Francis Portage. (*Lummi Elders Speak,* p. 64)

By the end of the nineteenth century, winter villages had been moved to the mainland, so exact locations of villages in the islands are not known. One village remembered clearly by Herman Olsen (an elder of the Lummi Nation) was in Mitchell Bay (just south of Garrison Bay). He recalls:

They had a nice, great big campground. Good camping place for the Lummi people. Canadian people and everybody were all mixed there. They had a nice big smokehouse built there; we call it a longhouse. There was about three of them, I guess. Then they had small camping houses that they stayed in. Made out of shakes and one thing or another, but they were nice. That is at Mitchell Bay on both sides of the bay. Those houses were known by the people that owned them. A white fellow moved in there. They homesteaded the whole thing. They just plain homesteaded it wrong and everything. Then on the other side of the bay, what there was left, the Lummis moved across, just a stone's throw across the bay; they had two great big houses there. Then they had some more small houses, cabin-like, that they stayed in that got homesteaded so the Lummis just lost out there too. White people came and homesteaded the darn place and never even left their ground for the Lummis. (*Lummi Elders Speak,* p. 66)

An offhand reference to a winter village on the northwest shore of San Juan Island appears in a written report of the 1860 Northwest Boundary Survey. On February 7, 1860, a member of the United States Boundary Commission described an old Indian house. The American surveyor William J. Warren was secretary of the United States Northwest Boundary Commission. He wrote:

> About 8 o'clock a.m. broke up camp and proceeded down the western shore of San Juan Id. Camped on the site of an old Indian village on the shore of a deep inlet or bay opposite the lower end of Henry Id. Portions of the old lodge were still remaining. It had been about 500 or 600 feet in length, by about 50 or 60 feet in width, and must have accommodated over a thousand Indians. As usual at such localities there were immense quantities of clam shells on the shore. (Warren, pp. 115-16)

No one knows exactly which bay Warren described here. People who sail around San Juan Island believe that the description fits Mitchell Bay, and therefore they suggest that the document agrees with Herman Olsen's observations as a child (Olsen was born in 1909 and Warren sailed in 1860) of the remains of a winter village in Mitchell Bay.

The next recorded observations of San Juan Island's western bays were made by the British in March 1860, one month after Warren (the American) made his. The British Captain Prevost was sent to San Juan Island to select a campsite for the Royal Marines. In his description of Garrison Bay as the best spot for the encampment, he made no mention of an Indian house or remains of a village at the spot. Nor did the British who landed at Garrison Bay on March 21, 1860, report Indian houses there. The site was described by Lieutenant Roche as "being well sheltered, has a good supply of water and grass, and is capable of affording maneuvering ground for any number of men that are likely to be required in that locality" (E. Thompson, p. 199).

That the American surveyor described an Indian house in February of 1860 but the British captain does not describe a house in March of 1860 suggests that the two were describing different locations. The American was camped in Mitchell Bay and the Britisher in Garrison Bay. However, one tantalizing fact thwarts accepting such a simple explanation. During the encampment of the British, officers kept notes concerning the work performed by the soldiers stationed there. The report describing the first task that the soldiers accomplished mentions dismantling an Indian house.

There must have been at least one house at the location where the British were building their encampment. This one house may not have been part of a large village, since these reports also mention the heavy physical work of clearing timber, indicating that the surrounding area was wooded prior to the British occupation. Yet, an Indian house was demolished by the soldiers sometime after March 1860. The report of the house suggests that there was some kind of settlement in Garrison Bay in 1860. Perhaps the house was smaller than the one in Mitchell Bay, or perhaps it was deserted earlier and all that remained was a small structure.

A Plank House

English Camp, as either a large or small winter village and whether occupied at contact or before, must have contained one or more cedar plank houses, each facing the water. Salish houses typically were 30 to 50 feet wide and 50 to 200 feet long. Smaller houses are known from Salish areas to the south (Puget Sound) that were 25 to 30 feet wide and 30, 40, or 50 feet long.

Two basic kinds of houses were built in this region: the Wakashan house type and the shed-roof house type. These two house forms were used by the Kwakiutl, Bella Coola, Northern, Central, and Southern Nootkas, and Coast Salish groups. A complete analysis of these houses' variations, distributions, and antiquity has been published by Stephan R. Samuels and Jeffrey E. Mauger as part of an analysis of the houses found at the Ozette site (45CA24) on the Olympic Peninsula of Washington. Mauger, in his dissertation research, surveyed all archival records of houses in the region and devised the classification of house types used here.

Ozette is the location of a historic village of the Makah tribe. Over 500 years ago (A.D. 1500) a catastrophic mudslide destroyed and covered at least eight houses at this location. The mud and water sealed the houses' structural remains, furnishings, and middens, preserving most of the objects until Richard Daugherty directed an excavation from 1970 to 1981 to uncover the spectacular site.

According to Mauger, Wakashan houses have low-pitched gabled roofs, and shed-roof houses have flat, single-pitched roofs with a low slope. The two house types have distinct roof support systems, suggesting that they originated in different places or at different times. Mauger points out that the distribution of these two house types is difficult to discern from reports by Europeans. Often gabled roofs were mistaken for shed-roof houses because explorers seeing Northwest houses for the first time mistook the low-angled gabled roofs for single-shed roofs.

This shed-roofed building photographed at the Lummi Nation between 1930 and 1933 depicts clearly how planks are suspended from and tied to poles to form walls. Note the split cedar planks at the bottom of the photo. These planks are split from one log using wedges and hammers. Myron Eells, who lived among the Twana and Klallam people from 1874 to 1907, reported that "the largest [planks] which I have seen were among the Clallams at Elwha. One was 2 ½ feet wide and 40 feet long, and another 3 ½ feet wide and 20 long. Such boards were split with wedges and trimmed by hewing" (Eells 1985, p. 71). (Photograph by Eugene Field, Special Collections and Preservation Division, University of Washington Libraries, neg. NA 1819)

Also, by the time that some observations were made (by missionaries and anthropologists), the makers of these houses had already been influenced by European construction, and were building their houses using foreign elements. The eight houses uncovered at Ozette are the only example we have of houses built before Europeans arrived. Many of the wooden structural elements of these houses are intact, and they are shed-roof houses. The people living in the San Juan Islands are described as building shed-roof houses that were in many respects similar to the houses found at Ozette. Differences between Ozette and the San Juan Islands are to be expected, but Ozette is here used as a comparison.

From Mauger's analysis we know that shed-roof houses were hung on a permanent framework of posts, crossbeams, and stringers. They had removable planks as walls and roofs. The posts were set into the ground with one row of tall posts in the front of the house (near the

This large structure was photographed on the Lummi Nation between 1930 and 1933. Note the dirt floor with the hearth near the back wall. Wide benches made of cedar planks ring the walls. The freestanding benches in the center of the structure are European in style and adapted for use in this large Northwest house. Not all houses had a dirt floor like this one. Al Charles (born in 1896), an elder of the Lummi Nation, recalls, " I think out at Village Point, Lummi Island, the bottom floor—the main floor of the dwelling—was twenty feet below the level of the ground, a deep basement below. They done this in case it was a cold winter. Today there are still big holes where those buildings were. They were in a shelter where it was nice and warm just like a basement" (Lummi Elders Speak, p. 64). (Photograph by Eugene Field; Special Collections and Preservation Division, University of Washington Libraries, neg. NA 1825)

water) and a parallel row of lower posts in the back of the house. Each pair of posts (one in front and one in back) was connected by a crossbeam. The roof was supported by a series of stringers that rested over and perpendicular to the crossbeams. The roof planks rested on these stringers, overlapping as shingles do today. The walls were made of overlapping planks and hung from pairs of poles pushed into the ground outside the wall. The planks were tied to these poles with cedar ropes and could be removed if needed elsewhere. Unlike the roof, the wall planks were not tied to the large posts supporting the roof.

The floors of both house types are of interest to those archaeologists not lucky enough to find a site with such unusual preservation

The interior of this Makah house also shows a dirt floor. All of the objects and food stored in the house demonstrate that, unlike the Lummi house photographed around 1930 to 1933, at the time of the photograph this house was still being used. There is a large hearth at lower right and fish hanging from the rafters. Mats cover the floor in front of the sleeping platforms. Note that roof boards have been pushed aside to let light in and smoke out. The houses found at Ozette might have looked like this. (Photographer unknown; Special Collections and Preservation Division, University of Washington Libraries, neg. NA 693)

conditions. If we are extremely lucky, the rest of us may find a floor of a house and use it to determine where the walls and door of the original house were. Most descriptions of shed-roof houses suggest that people walked upon earthen floors in the old houses. Dr. Wayne Suttles recorded that residents swept the floors daily with hemlock boughs, and sprinkled them with water.

Some houses, especially the Chinook house type used in the Columbia River area, were reported to have floors made of planks, which covered pits where food and equipment were stored. Dr. Kenneth Ames at Portland State University excavated a Chinook house near Portland, Oregon, that had abundant pits in a cellar-type arrangement connected by a central trench through which people could crawl. He presumes that the pits were used to store fish, roots, and other food for consumption in the winter and that planking covered at least some of the floor. The trench and pits had the feel and function of a shallow basement.

At Ozette the floors were covered by benches near the walls. The benches were not continuous and had large gaps between them, possibly to provide storage or work areas. Away from the walls and beyond the benches were hearth complexes containing ash, fire-cracked rock, bone, shell, charcoal, and burnt and unburned wood. The hearths were excavated into the earthen floor, and people walked on the earthen floor between the benches and the hearths.

The deposits found at Ozette are helpful analogs for determining if the deposits at English Camp were part of a house. At Ozette the midden was divided into floor middens and exterior middens, a dichotomy made possible by the preservation of the wooden planks of the house walls.

The exterior middens contained larger items than floor middens. These objects were often dumped in thick (1–4 feet; less than a meter) layers of highly similar debris, such as shells. Little other material was found within these layers, with few postholes, hearths, or laminated fine-grained sediment. These external middens, deposited by the occupants of the house around the outside, are thought to be dumping locations.

The floor middens at Ozette contain massive hearth complexes, thousands of post molds and structural remains, and large areas of thinly layered midden composed of smaller-sized items. These thin laminations, or layers, are less than an inch thick, lying one on top of the other and differentiated by color and content. The laminations in the center of the house were formed from a combination of trampling, sweeping, and oils seeping into the floor. These laminations built up over time to a thickness of 1 to 2 feet (.5 meter), depending on the location in the house.

On the basis of the descriptions provided by Mauger and Samuels, archaeologists should be able to recognize evidence of plank houses by looking for arrangements of large house posts, small wall-support posts, central pits and hearths, and different kinds of middens outside and inside the walls. Unfortunately no such unadulterated arrangement of house features has yet been found at English Camp.

One landscape observation missed by explorers and informants was that Northwest Coast houses were built on top of older houses. Debris was spread out around the outside of a house until the house was abandoned, and the people moved. People did, however, return to these older villages, sometimes after 10 years, 100 years, or even 1,000 years. They landscaped the area and built new houses in roughly the same location as the old ones, setting their new posts in the previously deposited shell midden. As subsequent houses were abandoned, the posts and walls decomposed. The holes left by rotting posts soon filled with the surrounding shell midden. Posts that decompose in a shell midden fill with more shell midden, and usually leave no visible record for archaeologists. The shell midden within the post's space looks the same as the shell midden surrounding the post. We have no historical descriptions of how house structures were abandoned or how new house sites were prepared.

Unfortunately most sites were not preserved by a mudslide, and it is usually difficult to differentiate one house (and occupation) from another. An archaeologist looks for clearly defined houses in a medium that is mostly jumbled. There are no precise answers to the questions, Where exactly were the houses? and How did construction techniques evolve through time? The midden at English Camp that is in the ridge and supposedly the outside of the house looks roughly the same as the center midden that is inside the house. The exterior and floor middens are clearly visible at the Ozette site occupied in A.D. 1500 but not as clearly identified at other sites occupied in A.D. 600 or even A.D. 1000 and left exposed on the landscapes.

EVIDENCE OF THE PLANK HOUSE AND
VILLAGE AT ENGLISH CAMP

The radiocarbon dates, topography, and artifacts suggest that plank houses existed at English Camp but changed over time. The earliest houses, made with shell ridges abutting three of the four outside walls, covered a small (almost square) area near the shore. Note the horse-shoe-shaped feature in the topographic map of Operation D (see p. 66). This way of making houses appeared around A.D. 600 and lasted for only a short time. People abandoned the use of a shell ridge around their houses, and by A.D. 1500 they apparently began making houses similar to the descriptions of shed-roof houses.

The horseshoe-shaped shell ridge at English Camp is one of the smaller houses reported for the Salish area. The shell ridge defines a rectangle roughly 30 feet wide and 45 feet long. No one knows the actual size of the structure inside the ridge, but if the shell was piled around the outside walls, then the house must have been approximately this size.

No houses seen or described in recent times have such thick deposits of shell against the walls. An exterior midden was noted at the Ozette site, but its thickness is recorded as about 3 feet (1 meter). The floor midden within the walls at Ozette is almost 1.5 feet thick (.5

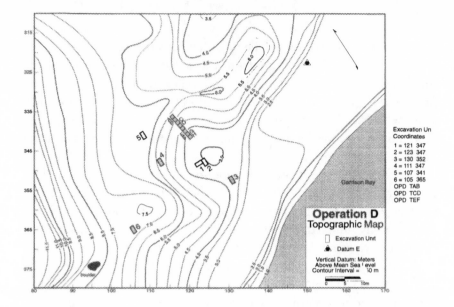

Excavation Unit
Coordinates

1 = 121 347
2 = 123 347
3 = 130 352
4 = 111 347
5 = 107 341
6 = 105 365
OPD TAB
OPD TCD
OPD TEF

This map represents the surface topography in the vicinity of Operation D at English Camp. Rectangles are outlines of excavation pits dug in 1990 and 1991 by the University of Washington archaeological field school. The area where the excavations are located is collectively referred to as OpD (Operation D). The contours are expressed as meters above mean sea level, with the highest tides reaching 1 meter above the mean sea level. Note the flat area just above the location of the shoreline and the wave-cut bank. This platform is bordered by a ridge curving in the shape of a U or horseshoe. This U-shaped feature is composed entirely of shell midden and is the location of a house structure built and occupied primarily around A.D. 600. The excavations were placed to investigate that occupation.

meters). At English Camp the exterior midden or shell ridge is more than 8 feet thick (2.5 meters), and the interior midden is 1.5 feet thick (.5 meters). The shell ridge at English Camp is considerably thicker around the outside of the inferred dwelling than the exterior midden found at Ozette.

Kris Bovy, a graduate student at the University of Washington, examined the faunal remains retrieved from the excavation of the shell ridge. About 41,000 bones were identified as bird, mammal, or fish. One way of explaining the difference between the ridge and the depression is to compare the numbers and kinds of animal bones found in each midden. The numbers of bird bones were so small that they could not be compared meaningfully. Only fish and mammal remains were found in numbers large enough to contrast the exterior midden (ridge) and depression.

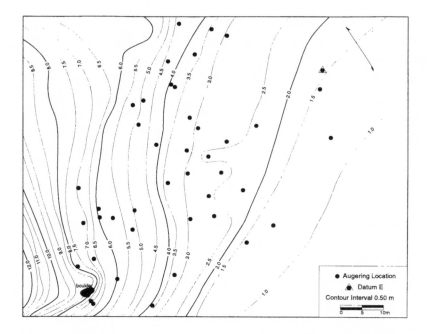

This map represents the ancient topography at Operation D before any people deposited shell. The paleoelevations were discovered by augering (at each dot on the map) to the base of the shell midden. The elevations were calculated by subtracting the depth of the shell midden from the surface elevation. Note that there is no wave-cut bank on this map to denote the position of the water at high tide. The location of the high-tide line is unknown, but it was supposedly further south (off the map to the right). The elevation of the high tide that cut the bank 1,300 years ago should be between the 1 and 0 meter contour lines. No coring location reached the depth elevation of the 0 contour line, so it was concluded that the shoreline was located to the south and has been eroded away in recent years. The paleotopography of Operation D demonstrates that a small platform was available for the first people to build a house and that the ridge built around the house was nestled up against the adjoining hill. Note that all of the shell midden is on a platform too high to be affected by groundwater or sea level inundation.

Units (drawn as rectangles in the topographic map) excavated into the ridge contained almost 90 percent fish bone and only 10 percent mammal bone. Units excavated into the depression contained roughly 65 percent fish bone and 35 percent mammal bone. This is a statistically significant difference. The unit in front of the house contained 80 percent fish and 20 percent mammal, a value halfway between the ridge and the depression. The single unit excavated into the area behind the ridge had the opposite percentages, with 10 percent fish and 90 percent mammal.

These data are difficult to interpret. Perhaps we could say that people discarded more fish skeletons in the refuse around the house, while mammal bones were brought into the house. This is not an activity described in historic or ethnographic observations of households. Fish—the flesh and the skeleton—were frequently hung in the rafters of houses to dry and to store. Deer and elk meat were also stored within in the house. But deer and elk bone were often used to make bone tools, an activity that might have taken place within the house. Few historic or ethnographic observations record where people dumped their refuse, so it is hard to determine the significance of where the refuse is, and what is in it.

According to one reference made by a Saanich informant to Jenness,

> custom demanded that the bones of all fish, whatever their species, should be thrown into the water, when it was believed they reclothed themselves with flesh and became fish again. Animal bones also were generally thrown into the water, not, however, to restore them to life, but to preserve them from molestation by dogs, which would annoy the animals' shades. (Jenness, p. 15)

Observations recorded by Jenness in 1934 may be inappropriate as a source for activities taking place at this house deposited around A.D. 600, and I have difficulty determining the significance of finding more or less fish relative to mammal bones in the ridge and the depression.

The function of the shell ridge around the earlier English Camp houses is, therefore, not known. Plank houses seen by explorers and recalled by elders had nothing abutting their outside walls and are described as being drafty. To insulate the living area in recent houses the wall interiors were sometimes draped with mats or tent-like curtains. Perhaps the shells in the ridge of the house at English Camp were used to insulate the outside walls and prevent drafts from penetrating to the interior.

The idea of insulating walls with earthen material may have developed logically from the idea of building houses below ground (pithouses). Pithouses were made by people living in the plateau (eastern Washington and British Columbia), especially in areas along the Fraser and Columbia Rivers. They were reported by Simon Fraser in 1889 along the Fraser River as far downriver as the town of Yale, British Columbia. Large pits were dug into the ground over which roofs, supported by poles and lined with mats, sod, and dirt, were constructed. These semisubterranean houses were warm in the winter and cool in the summer.

Some of the largest pithouses in the Northwest have been excavated by Brian Hayden along the Fraser River at the village site of Keatley Creek (EeRl7), British Columbia. A village of 500 to 1,000 people thrived there until approximately 1,000 years ago, when a large landslide blocked the water coming down the Fraser and disrupted the migration of various salmon for perhaps a decade. Not since then have people lived in large villages along the river. Instead, they have built small pithouses scattered up and down the banks.

Other people bordering the Strait Salish region excavated the floor before building a planked structure around it. Jeffrey Mauger describes various explorers' observations of a house built by the Quileute that had a floor excavated to a depth of 2 to 3 feet below the walls. In Barclay Sound, on the west coast of Vancouver Island, houses were described as having floors excavated to a depth of a foot and not planked. Chinook houses in the vicinity of the Lower Columbia River were constructed over deep semisubterranean pits lined with vertical planks. The Klamath, even further south in Oregon, also constructed semisubterranean houses with walls set back from a central deep pit.

Depressions, perhaps associated with constructing houses in pits, have been observed at the Cattle Point site and at a site across the Strait of Juan de Fuca, near Sequim. Perhaps the shell ridges found at English Camp represent early attempts to create pithouses above ground. The San Juan Islands are rocky with little sediment or soil cover. Excavating subterranean houses into bedrock at the shore would be impossible. "Depressions" could be constructed, however, by piling shell midden into ridges and living in the center. Perhaps the shell ridges at English Camp are an attempt by people to transport a useful adaptation from one environment to another.

An interesting suggestion was made in 1921 by Waterman, Barnett, and others that the shed-roof houses had an origin separate from that of the gabled-roof houses. These ethnographers believe that the people who speak the Salishan language moved from the interior, most likely down the Fraser River, and brought with them the shed-roof house. To the north and south people spoke different languages and made their houses with gabled roofs.

Jeffrey Mauger points to many problems associated with the notion that Salish-speaking people brought the shed-roof house to the Gulf and San Juan Islands. Many Coast Salish speakers build gabled-roof houses (the significance of roof construction is not known), and some non–Coast Salish speakers do build shed-roof houses. Until we understand the distribution of shed-roof houses and the importance of the differences between gabled- and shed-roof house types, the hypothesis concerning the origin of shed-roof houses will be difficult to test.

A proposal related to Waterman's, but slightly different, is that the first houses built in the Gulf and San Juan Islands (whether gabled- or shed-roof) were built above a foundation that was basically semisubterranean. These early houses were surrounded by a ridge of shell, creating a semisubterranean aspect. The basic Salishan-speaking people of the Fraser River built semisubterranean pithouses. If they were the first to move out to the Gulf and San Juan Islands, intending to live there over the winter, then the kind of houses that they would have built first would have been pithouses. Such a pithouse foundation is found at the Sequim site and perhaps at Cattle Point. At English Camp, perhaps the people modified the concept by piling shell around a central area, in essence creating a depression. This hypothesis is controversial and new and awaits testing through examination of more sites.

Whether designed to emulate a pithouse or just the result of piling trash around the exterior of a wall, the presence of the shell ridge in these old houses presented the occupants with some interesting challenges. The shell walls may have provided benefits to the people who first built them, but they also may have caused problems. Pushing shell against a wooden wall may have promoted rotting in a maritime environment. Walls would have needed to be replaced often if they were to keep the shell midden from collapsing into the house. If the shell midden acted as the wall of the house, as it does in a pithouse, then the shell may have collapsed too easily into the house, causing problems for the inhabitants.

Another possibility is that the shell piled around the outside walls carried water running off the roof away from the house. Shed roofs channeled water down the back of the house, and the water followed the contour of the ground, along the side of the house and toward the beach. Thus, water from the back of the house would flow along the sides, or through the interior, of the house. At Ozette, Mauger describes extensive whale-bone drains that functioned in this capacity. The shell ridge may have trapped the water off the roof, channeled it back and away from the walls, and kept it out of the house interior.

A third explanation is that the shell alerted residents that someone or something was approaching the back and sides of the house. Piles of shell crunch when stepped on. But was the alerting crunch of shell, positioned so close to the house, sufficient warning for anyone inside the house to prepare for an attack? If an enemy made it to the shell, then in mere moments he would be on the roof, through the walls, or in the door.

These thought-provoking suggestions (many made by the archaeologist Astrida Blukis Onat) are excellent hypotheses, and they guide us in collecting the appropriate data to determine why the ridges were made or, even more interesting, why the ridges ceased to be made. Up to now, however, no data have pointed to one functional reason over another for piling the shell outside the walls.

One last consideration that requires research is the possibility that additional houses had shell piled around them but that the ridges have been destroyed. The preservation of the shell ridge at English Camp is the product of not only the National Park Service's conservation effort but also the (unintentional or intentional) efforts of the Native American people living at the site. All construction of houses after A.D. 1000 left untouched the wooded area to the north. The shell midden in the Parade Grounds, deposited within the last 1,000 years, was affected severely by subsequent occupations. People returned again and again to the same landform of Garrison Bay, pushing shell to the side, dumping it over the bank, and digging pits and filling them in. If there were ridges there, they were destroyed. Distinguishing during excavation a flattened shell ridge from shell midden strewn around a living site is difficult. Nonetheless, the evidence suggests that the ridges were features of early houses and not used in more recent ones.

Some evidence suggests that before the British arrived a ridge of shell existed in one area of the Parade Grounds, the area of the formal garden. A photograph of English Camp taken in 1860 shows the marines building a garden (see p. 72). Men with shovels are standing on a ridge behind a garden as they watch men build a fence and hoe the ground. If the ridge in the photograph is similar to the one in the wooded area, then (according to the hypothesis proposed here) the shell midden in that one area of the Parade Grounds should be older than the shell midden excavated by Stein in Operation A and may be as old as the midden in Operation D, dated to A.D. 600. Excavations and dating could test this hypothesis.

Certain artifacts found by Sprague and Kenady, in areas away from the excavation of Stein at Operation A, support this hypothesis that parts of the shell midden in the Parade Grounds were deposited earlier than A.D. 1000. Six highly polished, ground, and perforated objects found during Kenady's excavations point to this greater antiquity. Each

This photo of English Camp taken in 1860 is the earliest known view of the activities at the encampment. The image shows British soldiers building the formal (or vegetable) garden. Note that people standing in front of the tents at right are much higher than the soldiers preparing the garden in the middle of the photo. The higher landscape around the garden may have been a ridge of shell that was leveled by the British during general camp construction projects. (British Columbia Archives and Records Service, Victoria, B.C.; cat. HP 12720)

piece is flat on one side, rounded on the other. Two adjacent holes are drilled from the flat to the rounded side. The sizes of the objects are all different, grading sequentially from less than 1 inch (2 cm) to more than 1 inch (3 cm). Objects with similar luster and of similar stone (although not of similar shapes or sizes) have been found at other sites and are thought to be part of the Gulf Island Artifact Complex. Such highly polished objects are found predominantly in the Locarno Beach Phase. The highly polished stone shapes are thought to have been decorative. Gulf Island Artifact Complex objects are very distinctive and pinpoint an occupation before 500 B.C. The nature of that occupation is unknown, but most likely it was a short-term presence involved with collecting resources in Garrison Bay.

The 1860 photograph of the British encampment and the presence of these carved stone objects, found in isolated locations within the shell midden of the Parade Grounds, suggest that people lived at vari-

These six highly polished stones were found together in 1972 in one excavation unit. Each stone has two holes perforating one side. The stones are flat on the back and rounded in the front. Highly polished stones made of this kind of rock are found in the Locarno Beach Phase, a period ranging from 3,500 to 2,500 years ago. The function of these six objects, and other such highly polished objects, is unknown. They demonstrate, however, the skill and exquisite artistic ability of Northwest Coast peoples. (Photograph by Nancy Morningstar)

ous times on the shores of Garrison Bay for a long time. They also suggest that an indeterminate number of shell ridges could have been destroyed by both Native Americans and the British (and perhaps the American Crook family, as well). Fortunately, the ridge within the wooded area was preserved and allows us to glimpse what may be the oldest plank house in the region.

EVIDENCE OF
SHIFTING SHORELINES

The relatively flat surface of the Parade Grounds is an unusual landform in the San Juan Islands and one that attracted inhabitants over and over again. Some of this flatness is the result of British and American landscaping, but this area was always naturally flatter than the rest of the beaches on Garrison Bay. The origin of the flat area is related to the manner in which glaciers sculpted the landscape as they flowed across the region, water scoured the shore as the ice melted, and ocean levels

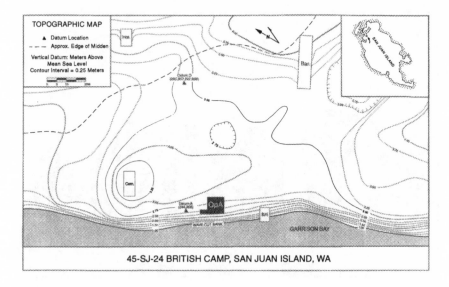

This map represents the surface topography at English Camp today. Rectangles are out-lines of historic buildings (B.H. is block house; Bar. is barracks; Com. is commissary; Hos. is hospital). The shaded area labeled OpA is the location of the 1983-89 University of Washington archaeological excavation called Operation A. The contours are expressed as meters above mean sea level, with the highest tides reaching 1 meter above the mean sea level. Note the bank cut by the water at the high-tide line. This kind of topographic feature, called a wave-cut bank, is used to locate modern and ancient high-tide lines.

fluctuated. Unlike the steep rocky slopes of most island shorelines, the flat landform at English Camp provided a foundation on which people could live.

The flat platform that made this area attractive as a place for people to live is cut on one side by the waves of Garrison Bay. Garrison Bay is ringed today by wave-cut banks incised by water hitting the beach when tides are at their highest. These banks mark areas of erosion caused by wave action. The Parade Grounds at English Camp have a steep wave-cut bank from which shell midden is eroding into the intertidal zone. Shifts in the elevation of either the land or the sea initiate the erosion.

Augering evidence indicates that this wave-cut bank has moved in the last 1,000 years. I drilled the shell midden with a screw-type bit and bucket auger. Elevations and thicknesses of the midden were measured across the flat platform, revealing that the old wave-cut bank was located between 30 and 150 feet (10 to 50 meters) inland from where it is today and curved first toward the east then out to the west instead of

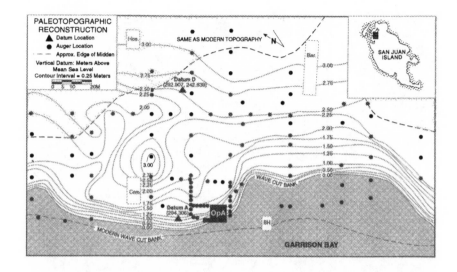

This map represents the ancient surface topography at English Camp, before any people deposited shell midden. The paleoelevations were discovered by augering (at each dot on the map) to the base of the shell midden, then subtracting the depth of the shell midden from the surface elevation. Outlines of buildings (as shown on the previous topographic map) are shown for purposes of comparing the modern topography and the paleotopography. Note that the location of the bank that was cut by the water at high tide is much further back than its location today and that the elevation of the high tide that cut the bank is at 0 meters above mean sea level, rather than 1 meter above mean sea level. These two observations suggest that the relative position of the shoreline has risen 1 meter in the last 2,000 years (caused either by sea-level rise or land subsidence) and that the landform above sea level has been built outward as much as 30 meters (most likely because people deposited shell midden at the shoreline, creating more land on which to live).

trending straight from north to south as it does today. Garrison Bay used to be bigger, and the platform now called the Parade Grounds was smaller.

When people first inhabited this level platform it extended as a small peninsula into Garrison Bay. People left shells and other occupational debris. Repeated visits to Garrison Bay resulted in people accumulating debris not only on the small platform but moving the wave-cut bank into the intertidal zone. The shoreline extended further into the bay and changed its configuration. Waves in Garrison Bay are not strong enough to remove rock and shell debris dumped onto the beach. These materials accumulated in the wave zone and remained near the shore, both above and below high tide. Slowly over time the edge of the

The sediment at the base of this profile is darker than the sediment in the upper portion because it has been wetted. Most people assume that rainwater wets sediment starting at the surface and that the upper sediment should be dark (wet) and the lower sediment should be light (dry). At many shell middens, located close to the modern shoreline, the opposite stratigraphy is observed. The lower layer is dark (wet) because the relationship of the land and sea level has changed over the last 2,000 years. The change has resulted in a lowering of as much as 1 meter of the land at the shoreline into water. This zone of saturation includes the lower parts of hundreds of shell middens. The water brings with it increased rates of chemical decomposition. The lower layers of shell midden are losing their shell to chemical degradation, and along with the shell goes the bone. In another 1,000 years we may have only stone artifacts left to recover.

In this additional view of Operation A, the dark layer is clearly visible on the bottom of the lighter-colored layer. Note that within each layer a variety of shell is visible, as well as small lenses with a matrix of tan or brown colors. The two-toned stratigraphy is observable only in a larger-scale division of the layers. The strings were hung at 10-cm intervals to assist the excavator in drawing the profile.

wave-cut bank was buried and the platform extended seaward. People actually made new land on which to live. The Parade Grounds we see today were made by people.

When people created this new surface on which to live, they also created a stratigraphic phenomenon unique to coastal sites but found all over the world. Many shell middens in the San Juan and Gulf islands have a black (dark) layer at the base of the cultural material, as is the case with English Camp. Various archaeologists investigating coastal sites in Asia, Africa, South America, and Australia have also noted this distinctive two-toned stratification and have offered plausible explanations. The research at English Camp was designed to determine, among other things, the origin of this stratification.

One explanation is that this two-toned stratigraphy reflects a change in people's life-style. The objects and organic residues that people first deposited were different from what they later deposited at the top of the midden. These early objects and debris turned the sediment black. Charcoal, if deposited in large quantities, could change the color of sediment, but no difference in the amount of charcoal was found in the dark and light layers of the English Camp midden, and few sites reveal any artifactual changes exactly at that boundary.

Another explanation for the black layer at the base of middens is that people living in all these locations threw debris into the intertidal zone, which is wetted at high tide and turns the large amount of organic matter that is ubiquitous in shell middens to a darker color. This still happens after a high tide. The shell midden exposed in the wave-cut bank shows a line of dark sediment below the highest point where waves hit the profile, and light sediment above this point. The dark color appears when the organic matter in the midden absorbs water into its molecular structure, changing its appearance. By the end of the day, however, with warm temperatures and sunshine, the profile transforms to a single light color. This process of wetting the lower portion of the midden explains the darkness of material thrown onto the intertidal zone, but not the darkness of the shell midden above on the level platform.

The best explanation for the dark layer on the platform is that it too has been wetted. The dark layer at the base of shell middens is wet because it has been lowered relative to sea level. This shift was caused by either land subsidence induced by tectonic shifts in the position of the land or by a sea level rise resulting from global warming and glacial melting. In an area as tectonically active as the Northwest, land subsidence is the most likely explanation. Recent experiences with El Niño, however, point to warming trends that could have raised the sea level worldwide. Either cause would shift the relative position of the land and the sea and lower a portion of the shell midden into the water table.

Evidence at English Camp suggests that an old, buried, wave-cut bank exists 1 meter below the elevation of the present wave-cut bank. The geologist John Clague, with the Canadian Geological Survey, has studied the changes in sea level and crustal movement in British Columbia (close to the San Juan Islands). He notes that various locations display evidence of being lowered relative to the sea by 1 meter within the last 2,000 years (but more likely within the last 1,000 years). The bottoms of shell middens throughout the San Juan Islands dropped 1 meter, some of them falling within the zone of high tide and groundwater. Before this evidence came to light, geologists had believed that sea level stabilized at its present position about 5,000 years ago. The minor fluctuations occurring in the last 1,000 or 2,000 years were thought of as too small to be of interest. Recently, with emphasis on neotectonism and global warming, geologists have examined carefully any change in the location of the shoreline and have discovered this small (1-meter) change. The evidence for the shift was always there, but it was of too small a scale to be significant to geologists. Only when the scale of their questions changed was the evidence observed. This is a good example in science of how the questions we ask influence the scientific observations we make.

The small-scale shift in the location of the shoreline over the last 1,000 years has influenced greatly the shell middens of the Northwest by creating a two-toned stratigraphy, of dark on the bottom and light on top. The lower portions of these shell middens are sitting in a bath of fresh, brackish, and salt water. When shell middens are exposed to water, the organic matter absorbs water (looks darker) and accelerates decomposition of the organic matter. The process liberates carbon dioxide and acids, making the water more acidic. The acidic water moves through the midden surrounding the adjacent bones and shells, attacking and dissolving their chemical constituents, and carrying away the dissolved components as the tide and groundwater ebb and flow through the porous midden.

Decomposition of the organic matter and dissolution of shell and bone in the lower portions of these shell middens continue until they disappear. Eventually the lower zones of such shell middens will be transformed into shell-less and boneless middens, which display a two-toned stratification of a dark layer (without shell or bone) below a light layer (with shell and bone). A midden with no shell or bone at its base, and abundant shell and bone in its upper region, might be interpreted mistakenly as the result of an occupation by people who used only lithics (tools made of stone). Additionally, a midden where the process has not completely eliminated the shell and bone might be interpreted as an occupation by people who depended on fewer shellfish and mammals than the people who deposited the shell midden on the top.

Identifying this process serves as a cautionary tale for future archaeologists. Shell middens in many parts of the world have been inundated by small changes in the location of the shoreline and water table. Landforms have subsided and sea levels have risen. Shell middens on such coastlines have their lower portions wetted by groundwater and seawater. They sit in solutions that encourage the decomposition of shell. Some of them have already lost all of their shell. A lower layer that contains no shell can be interpreted as never having had shell only after an archaeologist demonstrates that the layer is well above sea level and not subjected to this subsidence/decomposition process. The English Camp shell midden has this two-toned stratigraphy and is in the process of losing shell from its lower layer. I have not used this stratigraphic distinction to suggest that people with different habits deposited these different layers. I suggest instead that the level of the water changed.

Not all shell middens, however, are located close to the shore and thus affected by changes in sea level. Some landscapes on which people lived are well above sea level. These locations, and the shell middens on them, may have been lowered relative to the elevation of the sea by a meter, but the platform was too high to be inundated. These shell middens do not display the distinctive two-toned stratigraphy. Both the Cattle Point site and the northern wooded portion of English Camp (Operation D, where the shell ridge was found) are situated on such high platforms.

The topography of Operation D was different before people deposited the shell midden there, just as the topography of the Parade Grounds was different under the shell midden. The elevation of the land was greater than 1 meter above sea level, and there was a flat platform that was the reason for occupying that area in the first place. Augering determined the elevation of the base of that shell midden. From these data a paleotopographic map was drawn that depicts a small, level platform available for occupation, a platform significantly smaller (and higher) than the one in the Parade Grounds.

Reconstructing the paleotopography is something new to archaeology. The data provided are extremely helpful in reconstructing the changes that have occurred over 1,000 or 2,000 years. Campsites and winter villages on Garrison Bay were centers of activity such as constructing houses and processing food. Occupation by many people over many years changed the landscape considerably—add to that a complex mixture of sea-level and tectonic events, and one appreciates the difficulty for archaeologists who attempt to reconstruct the past. For these reasons, paleotopographic analyses have become crucial to identifying the context of artifacts and their relationship to behavior, landscapes, and climate.

TOOLS FOUND AT ENGLISH CAMP

At the winter village at English Camp, inhabitants manufactured tools, processed plants and animals for food, carved wood, wove fibers, and performed unknown rituals. Most of the objects created, and all of the words spoken, have disappeared. Some artifacts and features, however, have survived, and when taken together with the traditions remembered by elders, a vague picture emerges of life along the quiet bay. Of course Native American practices have changed during 1,000 years of inventing and adapting, and some details of the past are lost, but the reconstructions provided here about certain artifacts and activities give the reader a place to start understanding early life on Garrison Bay.

Procurement and Use of Camas

Camas is a bulb of the lily family that was dug by the people in the San Juan Islands. It is best known as the staple of the people in the plateau of eastern Washington and British Columbia, growing on prairies in dry climates. It was also important, however, to the people of the islands. Camas on the San Juan Islands was investigated by Gregg Sullivan in a senior honors thesis. Camas grows in prairies and southern-facing rocky slopes, encouraged by the relatively dry climate within the rain shadow of the Olympic Mountains. Native American informants remember traveling to the islands every spring to dig bulbs. Camas blooms in May and must be dug while the stalk is still visible. After the harvesting was completed for the season, the landscape was burned to increase its fertility for the next year.

Women dug camas with digging sticks. These sticks were made of wood, pointed at one end, and attached to a handle on the other. The handles were made of wood or bone with a hole in the center through which the stick passed. The handle was thus perpendicular to the stick and helped transform the stick into a lever to pry the bulbs out of the ground. Women preferred to dig bulbs on rocky ledges, where the roots did not extend as deep. In 1934 Bernhard Stern described camas digging:

> Diggers lay out little plots in the shallow soil where camas grow, cut the earth in small sections, lift the soil with the sticks and collect the bulbs in their baskets. They crush the soil directly afterwards and plant the seeds broken from the stems. Small sections are lifted consecutively until the whole plot is finished. It is customary for the women to return to the same places yearly. (Stern, p. 42)

At English Camp in 1970 a digging stick handle made of antler, with the head of a bird carved on one end, was found. Not much is known of the context of the handle other than that it was surrounded by shell midden and not associated with any noticeable feature. Although they are frequently found in sites on the plateau, digging stick handles are not often found in the shell middens of the Northwest Coast. None are reported in publications from sites excavated by

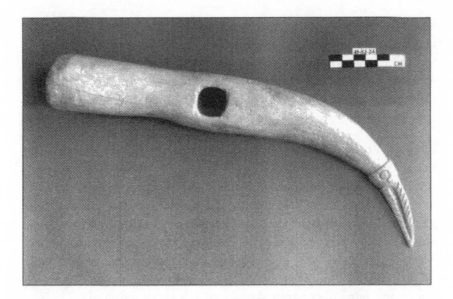

Digging sticks with handles were used to pry camas and other plants from the ground. The stick and handle were usually made of wood, but this handle found at English Camp was made of antler. Herman Olsen (born in 1909), an elder of the Lummi Nation, describes collecting camas. "All of those islands were covered with what the Frenchmen called La Camas. They are a little bulb. Each has a blue flower and just two leaves; one leaf sticks out on each side of the flower stem. They taste like sweet potatoes after they're baked, roasted or barbecued. We went out and dug them and we got a whole pile of them. We must have got four or five gunny sacks full" (Lummi Elders Speak, p. 56). (Photograph by Nancy Morningstar)

archaeologists in the Gulf of Georgia or San Juan Islands, although it is possible that some digging stick handles may exist in private collections. Also, digging stick handles made of wood would not have survived in the ground. The presence of the handle at English Camp suggests that women who dug camas brought their equipment to this site and perhaps processed the bulbs there.

Camas bulbs were usually stored in cattail bags after being steamed. Steaming took as long as a day and a half. If the roots were collected near the village, they were processed back at the village. If they were collected far away, then the processing was done at the collecting site. A Saanich women described the steaming process to Dr. Suttles:

> You dig a hole about two feet deep and about four feet across. In this you lay fine dry wood, then heavy sticks parallel across it, then rocks across the heavy sticks. Now light the fire. When the rocks get red hot this means

The excavation at English Camp uncovered pits such as the one in this excavation unit profile. These pits may have been used to cook camas. Herman Olsen (born in 1909), an elder of the Lummi Nation, describes preparing camas: "My dad came over and helped us build a fire in the pits; they used two pits. You go out there today and you'll still see those pits. There's a whole string of them on the beach because there was a lot of wood there to cook them with. They dug a round pit, and the pits had rocky bottoms and those rocks would get good and hot, but I don't know what they put in the bottoms of the pits before they put their bulbs in there. You cover them up in these pits, and you bake them until they cook good, and you take them out and let them cool off good. Then you can store them in boxes. You can put them away and they'll keep all winter. You just grab a bowl and go out and get a bunch of them, pass them around, sit down, and eat them. . . . We used to gather them every year. Most of the time we'd go to Spieden Island. You could get on the sheltered side of Spieden Island when it was blowing. We'd always go for three or four days and gather them. Everybody had a supply of them through the winter" (Lummi Elders Speak, p. 56).

get ready. When the rocks drop down, take the ashes out and level off the ground with a good hard stick. Then lay on kelp blades, salal branches, sword ferns, madrona bark, and the camas. With the camas, put all sorts of sweet bushes to infect it. The madrona bark and alder bark make it red. You must fix it so that no dirt gets in and yet leave it all full of holes. Leave a hole at the top and when it is all covered pour in more than a bucket of fresh water. When the water seeps through to the rocks, it steams up. Put

The Northwest Coast people used adzes to carve numerous objects from wood, such as poles, bentwood boxes, planks, platforms, and masks. The blades of these adzes were predominantly made of a rock called nephrite or jadeite, a hard green stone picked up as boulders in sediments left by the glaciers and quarried from (among other places) areas near Sumas, Washington, near the U.S.-Canadian border. This green stone was ground into long blades that were attached to handles made of antler and wood. As the adz was sharpened through grinding, the length of the blade got shorter and shorter. Most of the adzes found at English Camp are relatively short and may have been discarded because they could not be held effectively in a handle and still cut. (Photograph by Nancy Morningstar)

grass on top, then about four inches of dirt, then build a fire on top of that. Leave it all night until the next afternoon. After steaming the bulbs have to be dried a little before storing so they won't spoil. (Suttles, p. 61)

A pit roughly 2 meters across (6.5 feet) and just over 50 cm deep (under 2 feet) was found in Operation A on the Parade Grounds and can be seen in the profile of the excavation unit labeled 310/302. The bottom of the pit contained multiple layers of ash and charcoal, with little shell or artifacts. The middle and top of the pit were filled with sediment containing shell, animal bone, and organic-rich sediment, similar to the shell midden in the rest of Operation A. The pit is thought to have been a roasting/steaming pit, for processing either camas or shellfish. The stratigraphic location of the pit suggests that it was dug no more than 1,000 years ago.

These wedges made of antler were mostly broken, probably beyond repair, and thus discarded in the shell midden. (Photograph by Nancy Morningstar)

These two bits of evidence (the digging stick and the pit) suggest that camas was dug near English Camp, perhaps on the slopes of Mount Young or along the rocky cliffs on the island's western slopes, and that the bulbs were brought to the site and processed. Charred camas remains were not preserved in the archaeological deposits. These fleshy bulbs, however, decompose quickly once dropped on the ground.

Collecting Plants Other Than Camas

There is ample evidence that plants other than camas were collected and brought back to English Camp. Charred seeds of serviceberry, kinnikinnick, Oregon grape, salal/huckleberry, rose, thimbleberry, and elderberry are found in almost every deposit in the shell midden of Operation A. Margaret Nelson (an archaeologist working for Northwest Archaeological Associates, Seattle), who analyzed the remains, concluded that all layers have some seeds, but layers with abundant shellfish had fewer seeds of economically important plants. She interprets this to mean that layers containing 90 percent shellfish represent a specific activity, such as dumping shells after steaming. Seeds or products of other activities did not get mixed into this refuse.

Nelson also discovered that Douglas fir was the most commonly used wood (and bark) at the site, with hemlock and/or true fir also

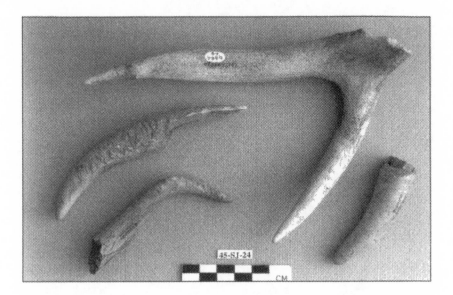

The tips of antlers, called tines, were found at English Camp. Tines are often found in shapes that suggest they were wedges, but they also were used to flake stone, and the tips were sometimes decorated and worn as pendants. (Photograph by Steven Denton)

represented in every sample she examined. The bark of Douglas fir was the most common fuel burned in sites where shellfish processing took place. The bark evidently burns at the most efficient temperature for this activity. Douglas fir has been described by Nancy Turner (an ethnobotanist working extensively in the Northwest) as the preferred fuel for steaming shellfish. It makes sense that Douglas fir would be well represented as charcoal in sites such as English Camp that contain so many shells.

Cedar was present in some samples, as was spruce, but not as abundant as Douglas fir. Western yew, the wood used for most handles, spears, and arrow shafts, was found in only 10 percent of the samples analyzed. The small amount of yew wood does not necessarily mean that people did not use it at the site to make tools during the winter months. Rather, it suggests that the wood was not often charred and therefore was not preserved in the shell midden.

Woodworking and Other Tool Making

The charred wood found in all the English Camp excavations suggests that people were bringing wood to the site for a variety of purposes. Stone axes, adzes, and other artifacts used to work wood were found in great

Abrading stones are often irregularly shaped: rectangular or oval with jagged edges or smooth ones. No matter what their shape, they all have one feature in common: a flat smooth surface produced by rubbing wood, bone, or stone. Archaeologists finger the surfaces of all flat rocks to find these smooth ground areas, which are the only indicators that the rock was an abrading stone. (Photograph by Nancy Morningstar)

abundances at English Camp, suggesting that woodworking was important. Adz blades were attached to wooden or antler handles and used to carve a variety of objects, such as house posts, canoes, paddles, and boxes.

Another important woodworking tool is the wedge, used to split wood. Native Americans describe using wooden wedges much more frequently than bone or antler ones, yet at English Camp, only bone and antler wedges have been preserved. Antler tines (also found at the site) are described as useful wedges and may have been used by people who made chipped stone tools. Tines are useful hammers for flaking stone.

Another woodworking tool is the abrader. Abrading stones are very common at English Camp and may have been used to sharpen wooden stakes and digging sticks or to smooth wooden carvings. Abraders may also have been used to sharpen bone awls, needles and slate tools. Finally, mauls (used as hammers to pound wedges) have also been found at English Camp.

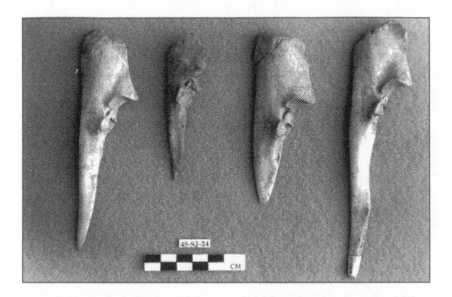

These four awls, made from the ulna bone of deer (the bone found in the front leg), are typical of those found by archaeologists in almost all Northwest shell middens. Awls like these have been used for 3,500 years and are still being produced today. (Photograph by Steven Denton)

Weaving

An object found frequently in Northwest Coast shell middens is an ulna awl. This object is made from the proximal end of a deer ulna (a bone from the front leg). The end of the bone is used as a handle, and the shaft of the long bone is broken and ground to a point. In all the excavations at English Camp, more than 20 ulna awls have been found, plus fragments with broken ends.

The weavers of the Twana culture group (living along Hood Canal, Washington), have been interviewed by Nordquist and Nordquist. They report that:

> the most important tools to the basketmaker, besides her hands, were the gauge and the ulna awl. . . . The awl was made from the ulna bone of a deer leg. The bone was sharpened to a point at one end and shaped in such a way as to fit comfortably in the palm of the hand. The awl was indispensable for most basketmaking and was an integral part of weaving. As the basketmaker twined the fibers, the awl was held in the hand ready for use in straightening and tightening the strands, for inserting new strands, and for tying the loose ends toward the inside. (Nordquist and Nordquist, p. 16)

Louise Pulsover, of the Skokomish Tribe, is shown here making baskets. She is holding an ulna awl in her right hand as she weaves the fibers. (Photographer unknown; courtesy of the Burke Museum)

These awls are still used by Northwest weavers, but they were not described by the early ethnographers interviewing elders or the explorers observing an unfamiliar culture. The reason for the oversights may be that the awls were used by women, and most early ethnographers and explorers were men. Male ethnographers likely had more access to the activities performed by men than those done by women. These ethnographers may also have been more interested in men's activities. Male explorers, as the anthropologist Helen Norton pointed out, were biased: they assumed that the roles of males and females in this newly encountered society matched the roles in their own society. They did not like to talk to the female chiefs, and they rarely commented on the activities of women.

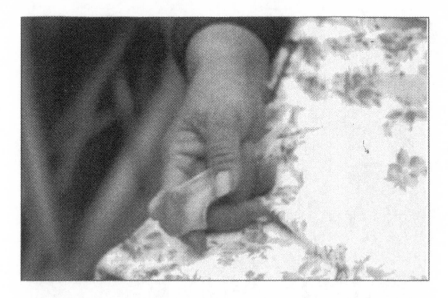

This close-up of Louise Pulsover shows the proper way of holding an ulna awl. (Photographer unknown; courtesy of the Burke Museum)

Photographed in 1995, this apprentice basket maker is using an ulna awl that has a very long blade. The awls found in archaeological sites have blades that are very short, perhaps indicating that the awl blades were worn away and no longer useful, thus discarded. (Photograph by Melissa Parr; courtesy of the Washington State Historical Museum)

An awl with a long point is being used in 1995 by Lena Dunstan, a Tlingit/Nisqually basket maker. (Photograph by Melissa Parr; courtesy of the Washington State Historical Museum)

The presence of the ulna awls at English Camp is consistent with the suggestion that the location was a winter village. Weaving was an activity that filled the winter months, and thus tools associated with weaving are to be expected at such a place.

Manufacturing and Utilization of Stone Tools

Before the introduction of metal, all knives, spear heads, tips of arrows, and blades were made of stone. Archaeologists refer to any stone modified by people as a lithic. There are two ways to sharpen lithics. One is by grinding a rock into a sharp edge on an abrading stone, much as we grind a metal knife blade on a whetstone. These are called ground stone tools. The other method is hitting a rock with a hammer stone (or antler) to detach flakes and create a sharp edge. These are called chipped stone tools. Both techniques were used to make tools throughout the Northwest Coast.

Thin sheets of slate were ground to create a beveled edge, easily sharpened with continued grinding. When Captain George Vancouver sailed through the San Juan Islands in June of 1792, he observed seventeen Indians: "Some of their arrows were pointed with slate, the first I had seen so armed on my present visit to this coast; these they appeared to esteem very highly, and like the inhabitants of Nootka, took much pains to guard them from injury." Slate knives and arrow points are found throughout the shell midden at English Camp, as well as at most sites in the region.

The other manufacturing technique, hitting a rock to create a sharp edge, is used only on rocks with fine-grained textures such as chert, obsidian, quartz, and fine-grained volcanics. Volcanics are the most common in the San Juan Islands. Edward Bakewell, a graduate student at the University of Washington, determined that a dark volcanic rock called dacite is the raw material of almost 90 percent of the chipped stone tools at English Camp. Elizabeth Martinson, in a senior honors thesis, examined all the quartz tools called microblades. These tiny quartz blades were made from quartz crystals found in volcanic rocks. They were found primarily in the deepest layers of Operation A.

Chipped stone tools occur in different frequencies at the English Camp site, and their frequency changes systematically over time. In the deposits of Operation D, and in the deepest layers of Operation A, abundant chipped stone tools made of volcanic rock have been found. In addition, broken fragments of the rock debris created in the making of the tools are everywhere. This situation changes in the upper layers of Operation A. Near the surface, the numbers of chipped stone tools and chipped debris decrease drastically.

The decline in the frequency of chipped stone tools and flakes is most likely explained by one of two factors. Either people stopped making chipped stone tools and replaced them with wooden tools, or people moved the place where they made chipped stone tools.

Replacement of stone by wood is not a likely explanation for the change in the frequency of chipped stone tools. Wood is not as hard as stone and would not be an effective cutting tool. If people decided to change from using chipped stone to something else, that something else would have to be as sharp and hard as chipped stone. At Ozette (where wood was preserved under a mudslide), 90 percent of the tools uncovered were made of wood, leaving all archaeologists to wonder just how much of the culture we miss in sites not preserved by mudslides. Yet even at Ozette some knives, spearheads, and arrow tips were made of chipped stone.

Perhaps people used fewer chipped stone tools because they began to prefer ground stone tools. Slate and nephrite have both been ground to form adzes and knives for the last 3,000 years. Some archaeologists have suggested, however, that the frequency of ground stone increases at the same time that the frequency of chipped tools decreases. At English Camp this relationship has not been observed. Ethan Cochrane, in a senior honors thesis, analyzed the numbers of ground stone and chipped stone tools found in all layers of Operation A. He found that, although the numbers of chipped stone tools decreased in the upper layers of the excavation, the numbers of ground stone tools remained the same throughout the whole excavation. Thus, the hypothesis that ground stone replaced chipped stone is not supported.

Another hypothesis to explain the change in the frequency of chipped stone tools focuses on a change in the location where tools are made. Archaeologists find the manufacturing debris of tools only in the places where people make the tools. During the long winter months of inactivity, stone tools were reportedly made outside the plank house, in the area between the beach and the door, or behind the house. According to one description, men went away from the houses and made their tools in privacy, so as to bring luck to the tool by performing the appropriate rituals.

In the deposits excavated in Operation A, the exact locations of houses were not discernible. Hearths and pits were uncovered, which presumably were inside houses, but obviously not the same house at the same time. The positions of exterior walls, doors, sleeping platforms, etc., are not known, and they probably changed over the 1,000 years of occupation. No evidence was found to suggest where exactly in the Parade Grounds a house, or many houses, were located. Chipped stone

Slate points have ground edges; dacite and chert points were chipped. Rock used for tool manufacture was acquired from the coast, the Cascade Range, and even the Columbia River. The kind of rock was crucial for making high-quality tools. Al Charles (born in 1896), an elder of the Lummi Nation, describes gathering special rocks for manufacturing tools: "They didn't pick up just any kind of stone to make tools with. They had special stones to do that; some kind of stones we don't have here. We went to the Columbia River with some of this food we had prepared and traded with the Indians down there. We got stones from them to use for arrow points, spear points. A lot of the equipment used for fishing ties in with the tools. They wouldn't use just any common stone for sinkers, for trolling, for reef netting, for any fishing equipment. They had to have a special stone that has a green and black color" (Lummi Elders Speak, p. 47). (Photograph by Nancy Morningstar)

tools found in the older (deeper) layers of Operation A could have been dropped in an area that represented the front or side of a house. They could have been dropped where people were making chipped stone tools or where chipped stone tools were being used in the house. Chipped stone tools were not found in the newer (shallower) layers of Operation A because people were no longer making them at that location. The place where tools were made shifted toward the shore, or to the side. We do not know where the inside, front, or rear of any house was positioned over the last 1,000 years.

This suggestion—that the Operation A excavation site was not the place where people made tools in the later period—may explain why stone tool frequencies decline in many shell middens in the Gulf and San

Juan Islands (it is a characteristic of the shift from the Marpole Phase to the San Juan Phase). At the end of the Marpole Phase (sometime between 1,500 and 1,000 years ago) people were living near the shore and dumping material into the intertidal zone. This dumping was purposeful and created additional landscape on which to build more houses.

At the same time that people were building the shoreline out into the bay, a shift in sea level occurred. The land, relative to the sea, went down. Houses situated with their front doors facing the shore (out in what is now the intertidal area of Garrison Bay) would have been flooded if the event occurred catastrophically. Or, if the event occurred gradually over an extended period of time, subsequent houses would have been built in landward positions. As sea level rose relative to the land, the shoreline began to erode. As much as 50 meters of shell midden may have eroded from a portion of the bank at the English Camp Parade Grounds. The bay is full of the shells and rocks that lay on the beach as the fine-grained sediment was winnowed away. Not only is the land going down and the sea going up, but the shoreline has been built out and eroded back.

In this scenario there was not a change in how stone tools were made, or a change in where stone tools were manufactured. There was a change in the intersection of the land and the sea: the shoreline. People's activities were oriented to the shoreline. A house was positioned relative to the wave-cut bank. If the location of the wave-cut bank moved, so did the house. If the place people made and used chipped stone tools was tied to the front, side, or rear of the house, then the place where they chipped stone tools moved too. Operation A was a single large hole that uncovered deposits of different ages. Each deposit is observed in relationship to the shoreline today, but that deposit may have had a different relationship to the shoreline when it was made.

Archaeologists often dig a limited number of holes at a site, often in positions near the shoreline. Excavating just a few units in a dynamic landscape results in sampling positions relative to the shoreline that may be drastically different from their relationship to the shoreline when they were deposited. Older layers were farther from the shoreline than younger ones, or the older deposits were part of the prograded shoreline and stuck out farther into the bay than the younger ones. Perhaps people did not stop making chipped stone tools; perhaps archaeologists have just excavated too few units to find all the areas where the manufacture of chipped stone tools has occurred. An additional problem arises when archaeologists do not use multiple radiocarbon analyses to date deposits, but rather observe that the deposits contain abundant chipped stone tools and thus label them as Marpole Phase. They may be deposits dating to San Juan Phase and represent a shift in the place where tools were made or used.

This is our second example of excavation strategies affecting the interpretation. The dark and light stratification was the first. One of the most productive research areas in archaeology is the investigation of the methods we use and their effects on our interpretation. These issues are hotly debated in this decade.

The two examples just mentioned can actually be combined. Confusing the whole issue is the fact that archaeologists collect chipped stone tools from layers observed during excavation—layers such as the light and the dark. The name of a layer is changed when some visible characteristic shifts, such as the amount of shell or, more important, the color of the matrix. The objects found in a dark layer or a light layer are then compared to one another. As I mentioned previously, the color of the shell midden is black at the deepest levels because the lower part of the midden is affected by recently raised seawater. The upper layers are light, almost gray. Previously, archaeologists collected chipped stone tools using these dark/light color distinctions, thinking that the color was the result of people's actions, not water's actions, and that the chipped stone tool frequencies are the result of culture change and not shifting shorelines and house locations.

The excavations at English Camp in Operation A demonstrated definitively that the darkness is the result of water saturation and that the shift in relative abundance of stone tools and flakes is independent of the boundary of the light and the dark color. At one location the dark/light boundary is above the boundary defining the shift in frequency of chipped stone tools, at another location it is below. In this case, the color of the layers is not related to the activities of the people who deposited those layers. Also, the frequency of the chipped stone tools is not related to the color of the matrix. Yet sites throughout the San Juan Islands have been interpreted as if the color of the matrix and frequency of chipped stone tools are related to cultural shifts.

At all future sites, we need to excavate broad areas of the site (not just one hole in one location), find areas with high frequencies of stone tools at the surface, ignore the color of the matrix as a grouping device, and collect large numbers of radiocarbon samples from all deposits. Only in this way will we truly unravel the events of the past.

Fishing, Shellfishing, and Hunting

Since the first Europeans arrived on the Northwest Coast, comments on the abundance of fish, shellfish, mammals, and birds have filled their diaries. At the Cattle Point and English Camp sites, numerous remains of these animals suggest their abundance for thousands of years in the past as well as for the historic period. The shellfish from English Camp have been examined by Pamela Ford (an archaeologist at Mt. San Jacinto College, California), who noted that all of the species in the bay today (and before the introduction of new species with Eurasian occupation) are found in the midden. Mussels, cockles, horse clams, bentnose and sand clams, venus clams, and barnacles were available in Garrison Bay. One shelled organism, the sea urchin, is not found in the bay (now or ever) because it requires a rocky coast with high-energy waves. Garrison Bay and the nearby Westcott Bay are low-energy environments with muddy substrates. Yet sea urchin spines are found in great numbers in all layers of the English Camp shell midden. Therefore, people must have collected them from high-energy coasts and transported them to English Camp. Such a coast is not far away, on Haro Strait to the west.

In the most recent excavation by Stein (1983-1991), millions of fish bones were collected in eighth-inch mesh screens. Peter Pegg, a graduate student at Simon Fraser University who analyzed the fish bones, has provided some preliminary information. The people at English Camp brought to the site bones from salmon, flatfish (halibut and flounder), herring (or smelt), rockfish, dogfish, and ratfish. But the dominant fish, by far, are herring and salmon. Fishing tackle, such as bone bipoints and pieces of toggling harpoons, are also abundant in the site, indicating the importance of manufacturing and storing fishing tools at this winter village.

Bone bipoints may have been important in herring fishing. Leo Senior, born in 1909, and Rose Senior, born in 1905 (both elders of the Lummi Nation), describe how herring were caught:

> I'll tell you how they fished for herring: they used this pole, kind of flat on one end; they used nails on it. I guess before that they used to use bones. They had a series of nails on the flat end of this pole. It was like a rake; they used to just swing this down in the water. Herring were so thick; put it down in the water and scoop the herring up. They would get caught on the end of those nails. They would bring them up and just shake them off and scoop them up again. (*Lummi Elders Speak,* p. 26)

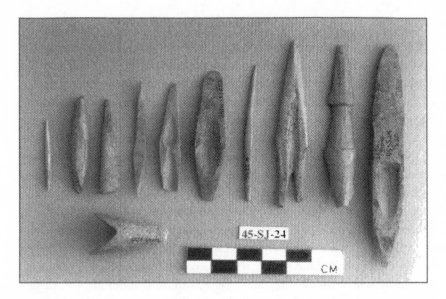

Most fishing tackle was made of either bone or wood. The bone was most frequently ground into points and attached to hooks, lines, sinkers, and bait to catch a variety of different fish. Some bone was used as teeth in herring rakes. Other specially shaped bones were assembled into toggling harpoons. Isadore Tom (born in 1904), an elder of the Lummi Nation, describes using wooden hooks and bone points to catch halibut: "We went out to the islands to get berries, and fish. We made poles for spearing fish. We made wooden hooks. We put a very sharp point of deer or elk horn on the wooden hooks. The wooden hook would float. The sinker would sink to the bottom with the wooden hook floating a little above it. Then the halibut who swim near the bottom would bite the wooden hook" (Lummi Elders Speak, *p. 32). (Photograph by Nancy Morningstar)*

The bone bipoints found at English Camp may have once been part of a herring rake.

The analysis of the many fish bones recovered at English Camp provides clues to the origin of salmon fishing in the San Juan Islands. What are the kinds and frequency of fish at this site, and how did the kinds and frequencies change over time? Catching salmon in the deep ocean is difficult without reef-net technology, and we do not know for sure when the reef net was invented. Also, salmon are only available for short periods of time during the year, making dependence on them subject to one's ability to organize and store. Other kinds of fish, such as flatfish, are available for more months of the year. People most likely depended on flatfish long ago, and then became increasingly dependent on salmon after adapting storage techniques and reef-netting.

These innovations may have been invented much more recently than we once thought.

Mammals were hunted extensively, especially deer and elk. Elk were spotted as recently as the 1800s, after which they were eradicated by hunters feeding the gold seekers. So many miners invaded the west coast in search of fortune that there was not enough food nearby to feed them. The hunters ranged far from the mining area and, evidently, were the ones who made the fortunes by feeding the miners. The elk, however, disappeared from the islands and have not returned.

For deer, pits, nets, bows, and arrows were the weapons of choice. According to Jenness, the pits were "dug about 10 feet deep along the animal's trails, placing in the bottoms of some pits sharpened stakes and notched poles for ascending and descending. The pits trapped far more deer than elk, the latter being, of course, less numerous" (Jenness, p. 9). Nets varied in length "according to the number of hunters, each of whom brought his own section to join those of others along the line of stakes. While some of them drove the deer towards the net, others concealed themselves behind it to kill the trapped animals. Then they divided up the meat more or less evenly, but the man in whose section a deer was caught could claim its hide and sinew" (Jenness, p. 10).

According to Jenness, "hunters who went out singly in pursuit of deer and elk often painted their faces with red ochre, or wore red caps; and they carried a pair of horns to plant on their heads in close stalking. To attract a buck elk they whistled with their mouths, to attract a female deer they whistled through a blade of grass" (Jenness, p. 10). Arrows were made of cedar "and winged, preferably, with two golden eagle feathers lashed on with cherry bark . . . [hunters] carried three kinds of points: a stone or mussel-shell point that disengaged when it struck, used for deer and for war; a bone point, rounded or knobbed to skip over water, for ducks, and a bone point with two barbs for other birds" (Jenness, p. 11).

Ducks were an important source of food as reported by both the Lummi and the Saanich. Birds were acquired in many ways. According to a Saanich informant,

> two men paddled out to a place where two currents met, for that was where the ducks slept. The man in front had a four-pointed spear that rested on a cross-beam and on some noiseless material set on the bow.

Although archaeologists call these bone objects harpoon points (a name that conjures up images of harpooning whales or other sea mammals), these carved objects were more likely used as tips on arrows designed to kill birds. Myron Eells, who lived among the Twana and Klallam people from 1874 to 1907, was told that the points' serrated edges were designed to catch in the feathers of birds. Wayne Suttles's Lummi informants reported that duck spears had four barbed points fixed radially. They were made of deer or whale bone. Two were six inches long, and the other two shorter; each had three barbs on one side. Some of the bone points had five barbs. The point at the bottom of the photo is unusual in that it has a hole in the end. Perhaps the maker of this point wanted to retrieve it after shooting it or just did not want to lose it and drilled a hole in order to attach a line. (Photograph by Nancy Morningstar)

The steersman sat a little forward of the stern; behind him a small fire burned in a wooden box filled with earth. When they drew near the ducks, the steersman muffled himself under a cape to resemble a stump and sat motionless, merely steering the canoe without raising his paddle. Then the man in front, paddling with as little noise as possible, speared the ducks one after another and drew them into the boat. (Jenness, p. 12)

Chris Victor Bosler (born in 1896), an elder of the Lummi Nation describes another way to catch ducks.

You know, my grandfather told me some of the Lummis used to go over to a place where there was a lagoon. It's still there but hardly recognizable. I saw it not long ago by Port Townsend. They'd go over there in the big canoes and they'd get two high, long poles with a net and they'd stand them up there just like you might a football goal. Then they'd get out there at the other end of the lagoon, take boards and clap them together and scare the ducks. They'd fly out to the big water, and they'd hit this net and get tangles in it. That's how they used to get ducks before they had guns. (*Lummi Elders Speak,* p. 31)

The bones of ducks have been found in the shell middens of English Camp. Kris Bovy has completed the identification of the bird bones, finding remains of diving ducks, dabbling ducks, gulls, and crows. An eagle bone was also found. One interesting oddity that she discovered is that birds are represented most commonly by their wing bones. Skull, body, and leg bones are also found, but in far fewer numbers than are the wing bones. She is now investigating whether this disproportionally high number of wing bones is caused by bone survivorship (wing bones are more dense and therefore do not decompose as rapidly), or if there is a cultural explanation. The evidence thus far points to the latter.

Carving Objects

Many bone and stone objects found at English Camp are carved. Although their exact function is unknown, archaeologists suggest that they were used as personal adornments. They have perforations in them that suggest they hung from clothes or around the neck, as beads and pendants. Others could be pins to secure blankets around the shoulders. Still others were carved for an unknown purpose.

A carved bone was found with an incised "classic eye," a form common in Northwest Coast art. Other exciting finds included a bone with incised circular grooves that resembles a rattlesnake tail and a digging stick handle (already discussed) with a carved bird head at the end.

One object of carved bone found at English Camp is shaped in a manner similar to objects on the shirt of a Lummi ritualist captured in a photo taken around 1933. The dancer's shirt is richly ornamented with beads and pendants in the shape of fish. Hanging on the front of the shirt under the beaded frontpiece are rounded spoon-shaped objects (made of either wood or bone). The objects seem to be hung to make noise as the person moves and beats the drum. Perhaps these objects were used in this manner for many hundreds of years.

Although we know the least about the function or meaning of carved stone, shell, and bone objects, they are the most delightful to observe. Bill Holm, an artist and Northwest Coast art historian, has studied the forms within Northwest Coast art, and Roy Carlson, an

The object carved of bone at right is similar in shape to bone objects hung from the clothes of Lummi ritualists shown in the next photo. One imagines that the objects would make wonderful noises as the person moved. (Photograph by Nancy Morningstar)

archaeologist, has traced these forms through time. Objects from English Camp have contributed to these studies.

CONCLUSIONS

Research conducted at the English Camp site has contributed significantly to the archaeology of the Northwest. Multiple radiocarbon dates illustrate dramatically the interpretive power of using many samples. Rates of deposition indicate that the horseshoe-shaped feature in the wooded area was occupied for a short time around A.D. 600 and that the rest of the English Camp area was occupied for the most part after A.D. 1000.

Close examination of the content of the horseshoe ridge and the area inside leads me to believe that the feature may have been the first attempt of people shifting from living in pithouses to living in plank houses. The piles of shell around the exterior walls may have insulated the interior from drafts, rain, or intruders.

Sea level changes were detected at this site that were comparable to those found by geologists. The discovery of a buried wave-cut bank in the paleotopography combines with other data to suggest that sea level has risen (or land level has dropped) almost 1 meter in the last 1,000

These ritualists are performing a ceremony at the Lummi Nation around 1930. (Photograph by Eugene Field; Special Collections and Preservation Division, University of Washington Libraries, neg. NA 1797)

years. The change dramatically affects all shell middens on the Northwest Coast by wetting their deepest portions with seawater and/or groundwater, thus producing a two-toned stratigraphic layering of dark midden in the deepest portions of the site, and light-colored midden near the surface. Archaeologists formerly used these layers to compare artifacts found in each, thinking the layering was the product of people's behavior. Recent research has proved definitively that the stratification is a natural phenomenon.

Artifacts from the various excavations at English Camp add to our information concerning people's subsistence. In the San Juan Islands, camas was an important resource that was processed both at the growing sites and at the winter villages. Berries of all kinds were important to the diet and were found throughout the deposits, as were the bones of fish (especially herring and salmon), birds, deer, and elk. Many tools used to work wood were found at English Camp, as well as tools for weaving and hunting. The richest examples of art were the objects of stone, shell, and bone carved (we presume) for personal adornment.

This information was gathered from English Camp incrementally, from the research of many individuals, and as a whole moved archaeology closer to deciphering the puzzle of the San Juan Islands' past.

CONCLUSIONS

People have inhabited the Northwest for at least 11,500 years. Today's visitors to the San Juan and Gulf of Georgia islands may not notice the descendants of these people or realize that their heritage stretches back so far in time. Often visitors hear only of the European explorers such as Cook or Vancouver, learning nothing of the first inhabitants of the land. The Native Americans know, however, that they have been here since "the beginning of time," and archaeologists add to this knowledge their evidence about the people who lived along the Northwest Coast.

Archaeological evidence is scarce for the period of time before 4,500 years ago, and more plentiful for the period afterward. The archeological record suggests that people did not always depend on the resources in the ocean. They did not collect shellfish or fish in noticeable quantities in the early part of their history, using instead the resources of the land (deer, elk, and plants). Only later did the occupants of this land focus on the resources of the ocean. In the last 4,500 years, the consumption of shellfish and fish increased greatly. The numbers of tools and strategies for exploiting the ocean also increased. The way of life of the Native Americans living here today is not the same as that of their distant ancestors. The archaeological evidence reveals some of these changes.

Two sites on San Juan Island, located within the boundaries of the San Juan Island National Historical Park, provide a glimpse of how people have thrived during the last 5,000 years. The Cattle Point site, within American Camp, was excavated fifty years ago using techniques that would not be acceptable today. Yet the evidence collected allows us to see that for thousands of years people came to this location during the summer to fish, collect shellfish, weave, and prepare food for the long winter season. Unusual stone and clay features uncovered during the archaeological excavations, and their placement and association with hearths and anchor stones evoke intriguing images of drying fish on the windy landscape.

The second site, English Camp, was excavated many times by three different archaeologists. The results of those excavations suggest that the landscape was a preferred spot for building winter villages. From reports of European explorers and memories of living people we know that during the winter Northwest Coast people stayed in houses made of cedar planks. The houses were places where food for winter consumption was stored, where weaving and other activities took place, and where multiple families slept, ate, and conducted ceremonies. Native Americans remember these houses: they faced the shore, and they had sleeping platforms around the outside walls, mats hanging from the rafters to insulate the walls and form partitions, and storage places in the rafters and the floors for food.

The excavations, however, suggest that at English Camp two kinds of houses were built. Over 1,500 years ago houses were square, with ridges of shell piled around three of the outside walls. After the walls either were dismantled or decomposed, the ridges fell in on themselves and left a horseshoe-shaped ridge facing the beach. This manner of making houses was discontinued about 1,000 years ago, and more recent houses were constructed without the shell ridges.

At English Camp, important research concerning archaeological methodology led to innovative conclusions. The dark layer, observed at the base of the excavation unit in Operation A (Parade Grounds), led to the realization that these deposits were inundated with water when the land subsided over 1,000 years ago. The elevation of the old wave-cut bank was a meter lower than the elevation of the wave-cut bank today. The materials dropped by people over those 1,000 years have been submerged in water to a depth of 1 meter. This submergence is accelerating the rate of decomposition of the shell and bone. In another few hundred years the shell and bone will disappear. The Cattle Point site and the shell ridges in Operation D were deposited on landscapes too high to be affected by this drop. They too experienced the subsidence, but it was not sufficient to drop them into the water table. The basal deposits in those sites are protected. How many sites in the Northwest have been inundated and have already lost the shell at their base?

Only part of what has been reconstructed at both of these sites depends on observations of the Native Americans living here today. Any reconstruction of 2,000 or 1,000 years ago that depends on observations from people's memories of only the past few generations is fraught with potential inaccuracies. Archaeologists find objects that no one can explain. We find features—such as the trench, clay bowls, clay ridges, and stone boxes at the Cattle Point site—that no one recognizes. These objects were important to their makers, but they are not used by people today. It would be impertinent to suggest that the Northwest Coast peoples did not adapt, invent, create, and discover. New ideas brought new technologies and improvements in people's ability to collect resources from the land. We may not be able to see the old ways: we can catch only glimpses of the differences between now and then.

Fortunately, the two sites within San Juan Island National Historical Park are protected from further destruction. The National Park Service is dedicated to their preservation and conservation. Thousands of other sites in the Northwest Coast are not protected. Urban growth in Vancouver and Victoria, construction of vacation homes throughout the San Juan and Gulf of Georgia islands, and shoreline erosion are all destroying ancient villages and camp sites. These sites contain materials that, in association with each other, could tell a rich story. They need our attention and diligence if the few that remain are to endure.

REFERENCES

Agee, James K.
    1987   *The Forests of San Juan Island National Historical Park.*
                Report CDSU/UW 88-1, National Park Service
                Cooperative Park Studies Unit, College of Forest
                Resources, University of Washington, Seattle.

Ames, Kenneth M., Doria F. Raetz, Stephen Hamilton, and
    Christine McAfee
    1992   Household Archaeology of a Southern Northwest Coast
                Plank House. *Journal of Field Archaeology* 19:275-90.

Bailey, Jerry W.
    1978   *Archaeological Test Excavation at Reid Harbor, Stuart
                Island, Washington.* Department of Anthropology,
                Western Washington University, Papers in Archaeology
                No. 9, Bellingham, Washington.

Bakewell, Edward F.
    1996   Petrographic and Geochemical Source-Modeling of
                Volcanic Lithics from Archaeological Contexts: A Case
                Study from British Camp, San Juan Island, Washington.
                Geoarchaeology 11:119-40.

Bakewell, Edward F., and Anthony J. Irving
    1994   Volcanic Lithic Classification in the Pacific Northwest:
                Petrographic and Geochemical Analyses of Northwest
                Chipped Stone Artifacts. *Northwest Anthropological Research
                Notes* 28:29-37.

Barnett, H. G.
    1955   *The Coast Salish of British Columbia.* University of Oregon
            Press, Eugene.
Benson, James R.
    1981   *Archaeological Testing at 45-SJ-274, Spencer Spit State Park,
            San Juan County, Washington.* Office of Public
            Archaeology, University of Washington, Reconnaissance
            Report 41, Seattle.
Blukis Onat, Astrida R.
    1985   The Multifunctional Use of Shellfish Remains: From
            Garbage to Community Engineering. *Northwest
            Anthropological Research Notes* 19:201-207.
Borden, Charles E.
    1950   Notes on the Prehistory of the Southern North-West
            Coast. *British Columbia Historical Quarterly* 14:241-46.
    1970   Cultural History of the Fraser-Delta Region: An
            Outline. *B.C. Studies* Nos. 6-7:95-112.
    1975   *Origins and Development of Early Northwest Coast Culture to
            about 3,000 B.C.* Archaeological Survey of Canada
            Mercury Series No. 45, National Museum of Man,
            Ottawa, Ontario.
    1979   Peopling and Early Cultures of the Pacific Northwest.
            Science 203:963-70.
Bovy, Kristine
    1998   Avian Skeletal Part Distribution in the Northwest Coast:
            Evidence from the British Camp Site, Op D (45SJ24).
            Masters thesis, Department of Anthropology, University
            of Washington and Burke Museum, Seattle.
Boxberger, Daniel L.
    1994   *San Juan Island National Historical Park: Cultural Affiliation
            Study.* Report 1443-PX9000-92-318, National Park
            Service, Pacific Northwest Region, Cultural Resources,
            Seattle.
Burley, David V.
    1980   *Marpole: Anthropological Reconstruction of a Prehistoric
            Northwest Coast Culture Type.* Department of Archaeology,
            Simon Fraser University, Publication No. 8, Burnaby, B.C.

Butler, B. Robert
    1961   *The Old Cordilleran Culture in the Pacific Northwest.*
            Occasional Papers of the Idaho State University Museum
            No. 5, Pocatello.

Carlson, Roy L.
    1960   Chronology and Culture Change in the San Juan Islands,
            Washington. *American Antiquity* 25:562–86.
    1983   Prehistory of the Northwest Coast. In *Indian Art*
            Traditions of the Northwest Coast, edited by Roy L. Carlson,
            pp. 13–32. Archaeology Press, Simon Fraser University,
            Burnaby, B.C.
    1983   Change and Continuity in Northwest Coast Art. In
            Indian Art Traditions of the Northwest Coast, edited by
            Roy L. Carlson, pp. 197–205. Archaeology Press, Simon
            Fraser University, Burnaby, B.C.

Clague, J. J., R. Harper, R. J. Hebda, and D. E. Howes
    1982   Late Quaternary Sea Levels and Crustal Movements,
            Coastal British Columbia. *Canadian Journal of Earth*
            Sciences 19:567–618.

Clague, J. J., and P. T. Bobrowsky
    1990   Holocene Sea Level Change and Crustal Deformation,
            Southwestern British Columbia. *Geological Survey of*
            Canada, Paper 89-1E:233–36.

Cochrane, Ethan
    1994   An Examination of Lithic Artifacts from the British
            Camp Site (45SJ24) and Discussion of the Adequacy of
            Culture Historical Predictions. Senior honors thesis,
            Department of Anthropology, and Burke Museum,
            University of Washington, Seattle.

Donald, Leland
    1983   Was Nuu-chan-nulth-aht (Nootka) Society Based on
    Slave   Labor? In *The Development of Political Organization in*
            Native North America, edited by E. Tooker, pp. 108–19.
            Washington D.C., Proceedings of the American
            Ethnological Society.
    1985   On the Possibility of Social Class in Societies Based on
            Extractive Subsistence. In *Status, Structure and Stratification:*
            Current Archaeological Reconstructions, edited by M.
            Thompson, M.T. Garcia, and F. Kense, pp. 237–44.
            University of Calgary.

Eells, Myron
    1887   The Puget Sound Indians. *The American Antiquarian* 9:211-19.
    1985   *The Indians of Puget Sound: The Notebooks of Myron Eells.* University of Washington Press, Seattle.

Fladmark, Knut R.
    1986   *British Columbia Archaeology.* Archaeological Survey of Canada, National Museum of Man, National Museums of Canada, Ottawa, Ontario.

Ford, Pamela J.
    1992   Interpreting the Grain Size Distributions of Archaeological Shell. In *Deciphering a Shell Midden,* edited by Julie K. Stein, pp. 283-326. Academic Press, San Diego, CA.

Hayden, Brian
    1997   *The Pithouses of Keatley Creek: Complex Hunter-Gatherers of the Northwest Plateau.* Harcourt Brace College Publishers, New York, New York.

Hebda, Richard J., and Rolf W. Mathewes
    1984   Holocene History of Cedar and Native Indian Cultures of the North American Pacific Coast. *Science* 225:711-13.

Holm, Bill
    1983   Form in Northwest Coast Art. In *Indian Art Traditions of the Northwest Coast,* edited by Roy L. Carlson, pp. 33-46. Archaeology Press, Simon Fraser University, Burnaby, B.C.

Jenness, Diamond
    1934   *The Saanich Indians of Vancouver Island.* Manuscript No. VII0G-8M in Canadian Ethnology Service Archives, National Museum of Civilization, Ottawa, Ontario.

Kidd, Robert Stuart
    1964   A Synthesis of Western Washington Prehistory from the Perspective of Three Occupation Sites. Master's thesis, Department of Anthropology, University of Washington, Seattle.
    1969   The Archaeology of the Fossil Bay Site, Sucia Island, Northwestern Washington State, in Relation to the Fraser Delta Sequence. *National Museums of Canada Bulletin 232, Contributions to Anthropology VII: Archaeology and Physical Anthropology* 32-67.

King, Arden
  1950   Cattle Point: A Stratified Site in the Southern Northwest
          Coast Region. *American Antiquity* Memoir 7, supplement
          to vol. 15:1-94.
Kirk, Ruth, and Richard D. Daugherty
  1978   *Exploring Washington Archaeology.* University of
          Washington Press, Seattle.
Logsdon, R. L.
  1975   *A Report of Archaeological Investigations, San Juan County Site
          45SJ169, Decatur Island, 1975.* Department of
          Sociology/Anthropology, Western Washington State
          College, Bellingham.
Lummi Elders Speak. See Nugent, Ann.
Martinson, Elizabeth
  1993   Analysis of the British Camp (45SJ24) Microblade
          Attributes and Preliminary Assessments of Gulf of
          Georgia Culture History. Senior honors thesis,
          Department of Anthropology, University of Washington,
          and Burke Museum, Seattle.
Matson, R. G., Deanna Ludowicz, and William Boyd
  1980   *Excavations at Beach Grove (DgRs 1) in 1980.* Report to
          Heritage Conservation Branch, Victoria, B.C.
Matson, R. G., and Gary Coupland
  1995   *The Prehistory of the Northwest Coast.* Academic Press,
          San Diego, CA.
Mauger, Jeffrey E.
  1978   *Shed Roof Houses at the Ozette Archaeological Site: A
          Protohistoric Architectural System.* Washington
          Archaeological Research Center Project Report 73,
          Washington State University, Pullman.
  1991   Shed-Roof Houses at Ozette and in a Regional
          Perspective. In *Ozette Archaeological Project Research Report,*
          vol. 1, *House Structure and Floor Midden,* edited by
          Stephan R. Samuels, pp. 29-174. Reports of
          Investigations 63, Department of Anthropology,
          Washington State University, Pullman.

Mitchell, Donald H.

1971   Archaeology of the Gulf of Georgia Area, a Natural
         Region and Its Culture Type. *Syesis*, supplement 1:1-228.

1990   Prehistory of the Coasts of Southern British Columbia
         and Northern Washington. In *Handbook of North American
         Indians,* vol. 7, *Northwest Coast,* edited by Wayne
         Suttles, pp. 340-58. Smithsonian Institution,
         Washington, D.C.

Moss, Madonna L., and Jon M. Erlandson

1995   Reflections on North American Pacific Coast Prehistory.
         Journal of World Prehistory 9:1-45.

Nelson, Margaret A.

1992   Shell Midden Deposits and the Archaeobotanical Record:
         A Case from the Northwest Coast. In *Deciphering a Shell
         Midden,* edited by Julie K. Stein, pp. 239-60. Academic
         Press, San Diego, CA.

Nordquist, D. L., and G. E. Nordquist

1983   *Twana Twined Basketry.* Acoma Books, Ramona, CA.

Norton, Helen

1985   Women and Resources of the Northwest Coast:
         Documentation from the 18th and Early 19th Centuries.
         Ph.D. dissertation, Department of Anthropology,
         University of Washington, Seattle.

Nugent, Ann

1982   *Lummi Elders Speak.* Lummi Indian Business Council and
         Lynden Tribune, Lynden, WA.

Samuels, S. R.

1991   *Ozette Archaeological Project Research Reports,* vol. I, *House
         Structure and Floor Midden.* National Park Service Pacific
         Northwest Regional Office, and Washington State
         University, Department of Anthropology, Reports of
         Investigation 63, Pullman.

Sprague, Roderick

1973   Location of the Pig Incident, San Juan Island. In
        Miscellaneous San Juan Island Reports 1970-1972, edited by
        Stephen M. Kenady, Susan Ann Saastamo, and Roderick
        Sprague, pp. 17-38. University of Idaho Anthropological
        Research Manuscript Series, No. 7, Moscow.

1976   The Submerged Finds from the Prehistoric Components,
        English Camp, San Juan Island, Washington. In *The
        Excavation of Water-Saturated Archaeological Sites (Wet Sites)
        on the Northwest Coast of North America,* edited by Dale R.
        Croes, pp. 78-85. National Museum of Man, Mercury
        Series, Archaeological Survey of Canada, Paper No. 50,
        Ottawa, Ontario.

1983   *San Juan Archaeology.* 2 vols. Laboratory of Anthropology,
        University of Idaho, Moscow.

Stein, Julie K.

1984   Interpreting the Stratigraphy of Northwest Shell
        Middens. *Tebiwa* 21:26-34.

1992   *Deciphering a Shell Midden.* Academic Press, San Diego, CA.

1992   The Analysis of Shell Middens. *In Deciphering a Shell
        Midden,* edited by Julie K. Stein, pp. 1-24. Academic
        Press, San Diego, CA.

1992   Sediment Analysis of the British Camp Shell Midden. In
        Deciphering a Shell Midden, edited by Julie K. Stein, pp.
        135-62. Academic Press, San Diego, CA.

1996   Geoarchaeology and Archaeostratigraphy: View from a
        Northwest Coast Shell Midden. In *Case Studies in
        Environmental Archaeology,* edited by Elizabeth J. Reitz,
        Lee A. Newson, and Sylvia J. Scudder, pp. 35-54. Plenum
        Press, New York.

Stein, Julie K., Kimberly D. Kornbacher, and Jason L. Tyler

1992   British Camp Shell Midden Stratigraphy. In *Deciphering a
        Shell Midden,* edited by Julie K. Stein, pp. 95-134.
        Academic Press, San Diego, CA.

Stern, Bernhard J.

1934   *The Lummi Indians of Northwest Washington.* Columbia
        University Press, New York.

Sullivan, Gregg M.
  1988   Camas Resources on San Juan Island, Washington. Senior
          honors thesis, Department of Anthropology, University
          of Washington, Seattle.
Suttles, Wayne
  1951   The Economic Life of the Coast Salish of Haro and
          Rosario Straits. Ph.D. dissertation, Department of
          Anthropology, University of Washington, Seattle.
  1968   Coping with Abundance: Subsistence on the Northwest
          Coast. In *Man the Hunter,* edited by Richard B. Lee and
          Irven DeVore, pp. 56-68. Aldine, Chicago.
  1983   Productivity and Its Constraints: A Coast Salish Case. In
          Indian Art Traditions of the Northwest Coast, edited by Roy
          L. Carlson, pp. 67-87. Archaeology Press, Burnaby, B.C.
  1987   *Coast Salish Essays.* University of Washington Press,
          Seattle.
  1990   Central Coast Salish. In *Handbook of North American
          Indians,* vol. 7, *Northwest Coast,* edited by Wayne
          Suttles, pp. 453-475. Smithsonian Institution,
          Washington, D.C.
  1990   *Handbook of North American Indians,* vol. 7, *Northwest Coast.*
          Smithsonian Institution, Washington, D.C.
Suttles, Wayne, and William W. Elmendorf
  1963   Linguistic Evidence for Salish Prehistory. In *Symposium on
          Language and Culture,* edited by V. E. Garfield, pp. 41-52.
          Proceedings of the 1962 Annual Spring Meeting of the
          American Ethnological Society, Seattle.
Thomas, Bryn H., and James W. Thomson
  1992   Historic Treatment of a Prehistoric Landscape. In
          Deciphering a Shell Midden, edited by Julie K. Stein,
          pp. 61-70. Academic Press, San Diego, CA.
Thompson, Erwin N.
  1972   *Historic Resource Study: San Juan Island National Historical
          Park, Washington.* Denver Service Center, National Park
          Service, U.S. Department of the Interior, Denver.
Thompson, Gail
  1978   *Prehistoric Settlement Changes in the Southern Northwest
          Coast: A Functional Approach.* University of Washington,
          Department of Anthropology, Reports in Archaeology
          No. 5, Seattle.

Turner, Nancy J.
  1979   Plants in British Columbia Indian Technology. British
          Columbia Provincial Museum. Handbook 38,
          Victoria, B.C.
Turner, Nancy J., and Marcus A. M. Bell
  1971   The Ethnobotany of the Coast Salish Indians of
          Vancouver Island. *Economic Botany* 25:63-104.
Turner, Nancy J., and Harriet V. Kuhnlein
  1983   Camas (*Camassia* spp.) and Riceroot (*Fritillaria* spp.): Two
          Liliaceous "Root" Foods of the Northwest Coast Indians.
          Ecology of Food and Nutrition 13:199-219.
Vouri, Michael
  1999   *The Pig War: Standoff at Griffin Bay.* Griffin Bay
          Bookstore, Friday Harbor, WA.
Warren, William J.
  1960   Appendix. In *Geographical Memoir of Islands between the
          Continent and Vancouver Island in the vicinity of the 49th
          Parallel of North Latitude,* by Archibald Campbell, pp. 115-
          16. National Archive Record Group 76.2, E198, Journals
          of Exploring Surveys, Washington, D.C.
Whittaker, Fran H., and Julie K. Stein
  1992   Shell Midden Boundaries in Relation to Past and Present
          Shorelines. In *Deciphering a Shell Midden,* edited by Julie
          K. Stein, pp. 25-42. Academic Press, San Diego, CA.

INDEX